BOOKS *by* VICTORIA HANLEY

The Seer and the Sword

The Healer's Keep

The Light of the Oracle

Seize the Story

How to
Write Fiction
for
Young Adults

Victoria Hanley

Cottonwood Press, Inc.

www.cottonwoodpress.com

ISBN 978-1-877673-80-1

Library of Congress Control Number: 2008921085

Printed in the United States of America

Cover art by Pat Howard

To you—
and your success as a writer

TABLE *of* CONTENTS

INTRODUCTION

Every Thursday at eleven a.m., Maryjo Morgan opens her home for a meeting of the Weekly Writers' Workshop—a group of people dedicated to improving their writing. Members range in age from late twenties to going on seventy. Each person has a different focus—everything from books for children to lifestyle essays to ad copy for carpet cleaning.

Some arrive ahead of the clock, and call hellos as the rest of us come in. Maryjo bustles in her kitchen, stirring a steaming soup kettle, phone wedged between shoulder and ear, finishing business calls as she nods and smiles greetings. When we're all gathered at her big welcoming table, Maryjo bangs her gavel—a gift from the group.

"Accountability," she says. "Who wants to start?"

And the meeting takes off.

Members report writing trials and triumphs: beginnings, completions, submissions, rejections, payments, contracts, leads—whatever's going on.

Then, before settling down to a critique session, Maryjo announces the weekly "prompt," a short writing assignment to be done then and there.

"This week I'm going to pass out fortune cookie slips," she says. "Take one and set down your thoughts about the fortune you get and what it means to you." The following week she might say, "Write about scars you have." Or, "Include the words *red*, *multifarious*, and *redemption* in a short essay." And so on.

She sets her timer. For six minutes, nothing is heard but scratching pens, giggles and sighs. The timer dings. We go around the table and read aloud what we've written, eliciting applause, an occasional tear, and sometimes gasping guffaws.

Often, the prompts that have been greeted with the most ferocious groans are the ones that yield the best writing.

* * * * *

The first time I attended Maryjo's group, I was ill at ease with the prompt. I was used to working alone within the dream world of the fantasy writer, and it had been years since I'd written any nonfiction. Now I was expected to organize my thoughts in six minutes, write them down and then share them?

Yeah, right.

When the prompt was announced, I sat struggling to find a link between me and my pen. Crossed out words soon covered my page. Sentences ran over and under each other, connected by elaborately curving arrows. What a mess.

But after half a year of weekly meetings, everything had changed. I looked forward to the prompt. Writing in the company of others took away the sharp taste of my solitude. And the chance to listen to an array of styles during the read-aloud portion of the group was a delicious treat. Also, my words flowed, sometimes without effort. Nonfiction seemed so refreshingly clear after a decade of writing fiction, groping my way through stories led by characters who refused to give me a clue of where I was headed until I arrived. With nonfiction, it wasn't a question of what I would say but only how I would say it. Cool.

Meanwhile, I gave some workshops about writing for teens. The young adult (YA) market was flourishing, and eager workshop participants were full of questions, so many questions it would take a book to even begin to answer them.

At first the idea of writing such a book was an easy joke falling from my tongue, but gradually I began to consider it for real. (If nothing else, having such a book would make it easier to conclude those workshops on writing for teenagers.)

The idea for *Wild Ink*—a book for people interested in writing YA novels—began to take hold and even seem possible. Naturally, I had doubts. Who did I think I was? Weren't there other people more qualified?

Well, I find that for virtually every undertaking, there *are* people more qualified. But I wasn't without qualifications. All three of my fiction books had aroused devotion in fans in many parts of the world. My novels had received awards and honors, perhaps the most important being an International Reading Association Young Adults' Choices Selection, an award that is chosen by teens themselves.

Besides, I reasoned, I could interview other YA writers and add their voices to my own. That would close gaps and bring variety, too.

I tried forgetting about the idea for *Wild Ink*. (Putting an idea aside can be an effective technique for finding out if you're really interested in doing it or not.) It went on growing, like an appealing weed, its seeds floating through the skies of my mind.

A couple of months later, I pitched the concept to Cottonwood Press.

The editor loved it. We were off and flying.

Wild Ink is not about writing technique. I won't be giving advice on how to chart a plot, tweak a sentence or refine dialogue. (Other books do a bang-up job of that.) Instead, you'll find info on the YA genre—with subgenres—and suggestions for getting close to the voice of your own inner teen. There are chapters devoted to getting past obstacles, and what to expect as you begin playing the publishing game. Editors and agents provide expertise about submitting manuscripts. And a third of the pages are interviews and writing samples contributed by other authors of young adult literature, authors who have developed winning stories. They generously give their best advice on writing for teens.

If you've been wondering whether writing for young adults is for you, by the end of this book I hope you'll have a good idea of whether the answer is "yes" or "no." *Wild Ink* aims to help you reach past limitations and get in touch with what matters to you. I hope it helps you explore unknown territory, tread risky ground, and bring buried dreams into the open.

Go wild!

Victoria Hanley

CHAPTER ONE

SPIRIT *of* YOUTH

SPIRIT *of* YOUTH

SO THIS IS ALWAYS THE KEY:
YOU HAVE TO WRITE THE BOOK YOU LOVE,
THE BOOK THAT'S ALIVE IN YOUR HEART.
THAT'S THE ONE YOU HAVE TO WRITE.

– LURLEEN McDANIEL

Is it me or is the world changing at a blistering pace? Inventions, innovations, discoveries! Wow. Much we take for granted today would have been considered out of this world a short while ago. Things move so fast that when boarding the light-rail for a trip across Denver, I sometimes wonder if I'll end up on a spaceship circling the Milky Way.

So how do we keep up? How do we write books relevant to young people?

I often remind myself that although the world changes, the spirit of youth is a universal constant. The desire to explore, the need to create new things and new experiences, the urge to express, to discover, to venture into the unknown—these are the marks of youth. Great stories for young adults bring forth that spirit. No matter the setting or circumstances.

When I'm asked why I write for teens, I reply: "I have my own definition of a young person: a person of any age who wants to do and will do new things, things with unknown outcomes."

Conversely, I think of an old person as a person of any age who doesn't want to do new things, but wants to know the outcome in advance.

I write for people who are growing, changing, developing, learning, taking risks. Such people are full of vitality.

Wild!

Naturally, there are as many reasons to write in the young adult (YA) genre as there are writers who do so. Numerous subgenres make room for scads of stories. The sky—or is it the galaxy?—is the limit.

That's where you come in.

Who Reads Young Adult Fiction?

Although the majority of YA readers are thirteen to sixteen year olds, people aged nine to ninety-nine read teen books. Seriously. Precocious nine to twelve year olds nearing adolescence are eager for stories beyond the middle grade (MG) category. And a hefty number of adults gravitate to teen fiction because they love the excitement of a well-written book with powerful story lines.

Since readership covers such a range, I don't think of a reader's specific age when I'm writing so much as I think about *coming* of age. And coming of age is a timeless theme, endlessly appealing.

Writing in the YA genre, you may end up touching the lives of more people than you dreamed possible when you started. I've received fan mail from Los Angeles to New York City, from Italy, Puerto Rico, Finland, Japan, and many other countries. Hearing from readers has given me a deepening sense of connection to the world.

Is This Genre for You?

What exactly defines a young adult book? A neat succinct definition would be misleading—like defining a teenager as "a person in his or her teens." But by exploring several consistent characteristics within the teen genre, I hope to build a clear definition page by page.

Let's get started by taking a look at the age of protagonists in fiction for young adults.

Age of protagonist. Protagonists of teen books are usually teens themselves, most often closer to seventeen than thirteen.

Does this mean you should worry if your protagonist is twelve or twenty-one? Not necessarily. The story comes first. If your story calls for a twelve year old, don't make her fifteen. If it demands someone twenty-one, don't whittle him down to eighteen.

More important than the specific age of your characters is what they're going through.

Coming-of-age. The overarching theme in young adult books is coming-of-age. Various premises are woven in, such as, "When the going gets tough, the teens freak out and then get their act together," or "Love is eternal even if it doesn't work out," or "Stand up to bullies but don't become one yourself." There are hundreds more, if we're counting, but the center of the story is still coming-of-age.

Formal definitions of coming-of-age describe the attainment of maturity and loss of innocence. Stories help bring perspective to the profound miseries and joys that come with childhood's end. Stories extract meaning from heartache and injustice. Stories transform fear and disgust into courage and compassion.

Fortunately for us writers, there are plenty of troubles and glories to go around.

Passion. Adolescence is a time of ginormous emotions. Remember?

Remember when a minor setback registered as an earth-shattering failure? When a C on a test meant the teacher was cruel to the bone? When a parent enforcing a curfew was an unreasonable tyrant?

When I was a teenager, the more I felt, the less I said about it, but some of my friends spread their emotions like spray paint graffiti for anyone to read. Whether teens parade their feelings or not, most can go from eager to apathetic, easygoing to raging, buoyant to downcast, all in the course of a day. You name it, teens have felt it. Emotions ebb and flow like tides—rip tides, not feeble ripples. Deep and strong. Passionate.

Stories about restrained characters being reasonable won't hold interest for teens. In the YA genre, tame is lame. So write with passion. If you're a passionate person, more power to you—and more joy, despair, fury, tenderness, thrills, chills, fire. And love.

Honesty. Want the truth? Blunt, in-your-face, stripped down? Ask a teen.

Ruthless brutal honesty may be hard to take sometimes—such as, for me, in the morning before the cotton in my head has been replaced with a brain—but overall it's enlivening. Do you think so, too? If not, this might be a good place to ask: Do you like teenagers? (If you don't, you might want to try a different genre.)

Independence. Why is the protagonist of a young adult detective novel going to be a teenager? Because adults stepping in to solve the crime would ruin everything.

Adolescents reaching for adulthood are seeking independence. They can't get there letting adults handle their problems. Confronting and resolving their own conflicts, enduring their own heartaches, recovering from their own stumbles, is empowering. Books that show the painful joy of moving from dependence to self-reliance are likewise empowering.

Whatever the trouble is, let the young characters deal with it. Can they occasionally consult a wise mentor? Sure. But the answers they receive should not be easy to apply. In fiction, mentors use riddles or give advice that's quickly forgotten or seems impossible to follow. Sometimes the advice is wrong altogether—or the mentor who is supposed to save the day is called away at a crucial moment.

Adolescent rebellion goes hand in hand with the urge for independence. Teens rebelling against authority don't see themselves as typical "rebellious teenagers." For them, it's all about a fresh perspective. It's about throwing off arbitrary rules made by narrow-minded sticklers or unimaginative fuddy-duddies. Why should they do something a certain way just because it's been done that way a hundred times before? Why should they bow to an authority they despise? Why allow anyone to tell them what to do?

Themes of rebellion against unreasonable or tyrannical people and situations are always popular in YA books. Readers identify with teen protagonists who break free.

Wild exploration. Think back on your wildest moments. Did you, like me, take a flying leap from one rooftop to another? Jump from a ridiculously high spire of rock into a pool of water? Get on your bike and glide down the steepest hills you could find while perched precariously on the seat, feet propped on the handlebars?

Taking those actions (and many others) did not reflect the best judgment. But what fun! Risks seemed trivial. The thrill was what mattered.

How about you? How about the people you know?

For many, our wildest and craziest actions are taken during our teen years or early twenties. Neurologists tell us the adolescent brain is a work in progress, a stage of life guided by emotion more than reason, when bouts of recklessness are likely. History tells us adolescence is a time of exploration.

Some explorations work out fantastically well. The rush of discovery, of breaking new ground, of rising to a challenge, can help launch fulfilling journeys, splendid careers, profound relationships.

At the other end of the spectrum, some explorations result in lasting injury. We've all known—or been—people who took risks involving drugs, alcohol, sex, speeding, fighting, etc.

Teens are experiencing the parts of life that are dark and sad as well as uplifting. Authors writing for teens do not gloss over jagged edges. In teen literature, sometimes people die or change so drastically that nothing will ever be the same. Love is tested against the world, and hope must survive reality. Wounds leave scars. Prices are paid. Authors confront the frustrations and embarrassments, mistakes and unwanted consequences that are part of growing up.

Ask yourself if you as a writer are willing to take on things that aren't pretty and don't resolve easily.

Breakdown/breakthrough. Breakdown. Haven't we all been through about four thousand moments when things seem truly terrible—when situations feel like burning debris falling on our heads, when our sense of perspective is dim and skewed, when hopes and dreams collapse like the Twin Towers?

Then there's breakthrough. The uplifting "ah-ha" that enables fresh understanding, the sudden giggle as we laugh at ourselves, the mysterious inner change giving us a second wind at the end of our strength.

I'm not a psychologist, but anecdotal research tells me that *breakdown* is often paired with *breakthrough*. Speaking for myself, it's when I reach a dead end that it occurs to me to turn around. And when the pit of despair yawns in my face, I know it's time to wake up and do things differently.

I may—oh, let's be honest, I *will*—crash into a few walls before I find the open door, cry before I smile, feel dark and lost before the lights go on and show me where I am. But I've come to know that when I'm praying for perspective, it's going to dawn. Eventually. In my life, breaking down and breaking through are two sides of the same crater.

Breakdowns and breakthroughs seem to be more frequent in the lives of those who want to do and *will* do new things. Learning curves are steep and fast. Hormones are racing. Inner life is stretching and reaching for what's next. Much is outgrown, and much more grown into—and then outgrown again. New tastes are discovered and discarded. Dire dejection meets outrageous comedy. Hope and angst. Idealism, cynicism.

Everything is going on.

And this is the stuff of marvelous stories! Think about it—would you rather read about someone who walked through an open door, or someone who found an open door after crashing into seven walls? Would you rather hear about a quarterback whose every pass was caught and whose team sailed easily to victory after victory, or about a badly injured quarterback who persisted through recovery to lead his team again? Would you rather read about a romance that runs a smooth course from minute to minute and week to week, or a romance that falls like a massive meteorite, opening a lava pit from which the hero must crawl to find a new love that heals the day?

Breakdown and breakthrough, struggles for independence, wild times, honesty and passion—when you put all these elements into your story, you're well on your way to writing YA fiction that will appeal to teens.

Length and Style in YA Books

Page requirements for teen titles used to be strict. Roughly 60,000 words was the norm. Those requirements have loosened up, and now teen books can range from just short of a hundred pages to over six hundred. Lots of leeway.

In general, teen lit moves at a brisk pace. Compared with traditional adult fiction, everything's a bit more condensed and intense, like the lives of those coming of age. Aim for a style that keeps pace with your readers, a style that emphasizes a strong voice.

Do you restrict vocabulary for teens, using only words readers are sure to be familiar with? No. Personally, I use the word the story calls for, whether that word has two syllables or five. No one complains that I use too many big words. (If you're wondering about profanity, it's addressed later in this chapter.)

What about keeping up with technology, fashion, and slang? A valid question. Language is on the move. (The website urbandictionary.com has over a million entries and counting.) When writing about gadgets, outfits, or ways of speaking, it's disconcerting to realize they could all slide into the past faster than you can say "dude."

My best advice for this problem is to focus on the story first, remembering that the essence of a person's life—or story about it—will never be defined by the latest tech-toy, style, or slang. It's neither necessary nor possible for our writing to reflect a reader's up-to-the-minute environment. Most books are published years after being submitted by the author, during which time technology will have advanced, styles will have changed, and slang will have fallen out of favor. If the story's good, however, readers won't fixate on whether the book is totally current. Slang may go in and out, but stories are forever.

Still, it's a good idea to keep in mind, as you write, that change is rapid in this day and age. You may want to skip using the latest and greatest slang word in a character's speech, while still being true to a teen's casual way of speaking. Too much slang can quickly make your work sound dated.

If you're afraid you can't do justice to modern times, consider writing a book set in the future—where you get to make up the terminology. Or try the past, so research can guide you about trends and slang. Or fantasy, where anything goes.

Sci-fi, historical fiction, fantasy. We've arrived at the topic of subgenres.

YA Subgenres

There are several zillion subgenres in the young adult category. (By the time this book is published, there may be more.) We'll look at a variety, to give you a sense of which type(s) may best suit your writing style. Each has its own characteristics and its own fans, and each requires something a little different from writers.

Contemporary. Contemporary YA is the broadest of the subgenre categories, encompassing characters who face just about every issue you can name. As always, the overarching theme is coming of age. Set in the modern world, contemporary books most often emphasize character growth in a context of relationship with others, with self, and with the world.

In the area of personal relationships you'll find teen protagonists interacting with friends, teachers, parents, siblings, relatives, step-families, love interests. Characters may find themselves growing away from friends who were once close, or living in a family where the parents are ready to divorce. They may fight with their siblings, hate their teachers, feel the pain of betrayal by a loved one. By the end of the book, some of the conflict will be resolved as characters grow and change. They may find new friends, discover a mentor, ease a tense relationship with a parent or stepparent, begin to value the sibling they used to fight with daily, or get over a broken heart.

Regarding relationships with self, teen characters may be shown struggling to sort out matters of identity, including racial, cultural, and gender identity or sexual orientation. They may be seeking an absent parent or exploring what it means to them to be adopted. They may be struggling with issues of peer pressure, conscience, personality, or self-esteem. Another popular theme is dreams and ambitions in stories of talented teen musicians, actors, dancers, painters, writers, athletes.

Issues involving health and well-being have also found their way into contemporary novels for young adults, showing teens who are dealing with diseases, handicaps, injuries, stress, depression, suicide, self-mutilation, and problems with drug and alcohol addictions.

Experiences with the outer world in its harshest or most challenging forms are also explored. Stories can detail great hardships, including being involved in intense competition, getting bullied or treated like an outcast, suffering physical and/or sexual abuse, enduring gang wars, terrorism, environmental disasters.

And of course there are stories that highlight dating, awakening sexuality, and everything that goes along with surging hormones, from feverish excitement over a single kiss to unplanned pregnancies.

The themes listed in the above paragraphs show how many experiences teen protagonists may have in the course of a contemporary novel. It's a long list, and by no means complete. When deciding whether to write in this subgenre, your own passionate interests will guide you. You can draw on your understanding of life. If your father was an alcoholic and you started sneaking booze as a teenager, you can mine the experience to create a novel where alcoholism is part of the story. If you've been active in politics, your book could have a student running for office. If you've been in the foster care system, you can tell it like it is. No matter where your life has led, it can enrich your writing.

Multicultural. Teens coming to terms with cultural differences create a perfect forum for stories that show characters learning about themselves, where they come from, who they are, and where they're going.

Sometimes the emphasis of a multicultural story is about clashes between parents who want to preserve the customs of their culture of origin and teenage children who don't. Sometimes it's about learning to value a heritage that has almost been lost. It might be concerned with feelings of displacement or loneliness within a community where the protagonist is not welcome. It might be about dating someone from a different ethnic group or religion. The possibilities are endless.

African American, Native American, Asian American, and Latino American multicultural stories have some representation in YA literature—though not enough. And there's a lot of diversity among immigrant populations that isn't yet represented at the YA table at all.

Besides ethnic groups, multicultural literature can also address differences in religious backgrounds. There's wide territory here for writing books that give readers more awareness.

In the U.S., more and more children of marriages that unite people of different faiths or races are growing up. These young people are eager to find voices with whom they can relate. If you have a background in or affinity for any of these diverse groups, you can add your perspective to the growing body of multicultural literature within YA.

Gay, lesbian, bisexual, transgender, queer or questioning (GLBTQ).

This category is familiar to teen librarians across the U.S., and encompasses just what it says: literature about teens who are gay or lesbian, teens who are bisexual, teens who identify with their opposite gender, or those who are simply questioning their sexual identity.

Within GLBTQ, the larger subcategory is Gay and Lesbian (GL). Teens search out books with protagonists they can relate to, protagonists finding self-acceptance and living their lives.

Fantasy. Fantasies are set in imaginary worlds or introduce imaginary elements into the world we know. In "traditional" fantasy, the world is dreamed up by the author, though it may contain elements drawn from historical times on earth. "Urban" fantasy can be set in modern cities or futuristic places.

These books usually include plenty of adventure. Magicians, elves, dragons. Crystal balls, magic swords, enchanted islands. Anything is possible—any creature can come to life, any item can store special powers. Wizards, sorcerers, seers and the like often interact with regular humans.

If technology is present, it's secondary to the central action and never used to solve the central conflict. This is an important identifying mark of fantasy. Spiritual insight, magical power, or strong character traits must solve the central conflict. (This contrasts with science fiction, a genre in which the right piece of technology or the right scientific formula may well be the hero's quest because if found it can solve the central problem.)

Modern coming-of-age issues can be treated in an allegorical way in YA fantasy. For example, the story of a hero who has lost his father, his kingdom, and his freedom, is the story of any young person whose world has been turned upside down.

The plight of a gifted young woman in a fantasy realm who is shunned because of her background applies to modern teens who are treated as outcasts because of where they come from.

All genres require the writer to successfully suspend the reader's disbelief, but your job as a fantasy writer involves extra work. Along with a good story you must weave a convincing world, a world where characters and circumstances behave in ways not seen in normal life. You must portray magic as if it's part of ordinary reality.

I write fantasy. When I was growing up, every week I came up with some new escapist daydream about other worlds. In school I'd hide books like *The Lord of the Rings* inside my chemistry book. How about you? Does your mind take you on similar excursions? Would you like to bring other people with you? The magic of words is your ticket. My best advice for writing fantasy is to believe what you're writing about—while you're writing, that is.

Science fiction.
In the adult fiction section of libraries, sci-fi books are found spine to spine with fantasy. Both are considered highly imaginative genres; both create worlds that do not actually exist. But the worlds found in sci-fi novels are linked to scientific principles. Instead of sorcerers, robots. Instead of telepathy, radar. Instead of crystal balls, statistical analysis. Science fiction is almost always set in the future, and technology is almost always central to the action.

However, sometimes sci-fi and fantasy blend together: wizards may battle extraordinary machines, dragons may breathe fire over a settlement on a foreign world, a teen who can shape-change may be fitted with a nano-chip that inhibits her powers.

Such things would not happen in "hard" sci-fi, which is based firmly upon scientific knowledge. Hard sci-fi writers have studied physics, and they don't deviate from the parameters set by established science. Their stories may fly through outer space, or perhaps into a parallel universe—but only because they believe space travel and parallel travel are logical extensions of today's scientific achievements.

In YA sci-fi, teen protagonists must keep their nerve in the face of daunting circumstances—they must use their thinking powers to discover solutions. In the hands of an ingenious writer, the coming-of-age theme works well within a sci-fi story.

It takes a particular personality to come up with believable future scenarios and inventive technologies. Are you a dedicated scientific thinker? Are you always reading up on new discoveries? Are science pages bookmarked on your computer? You could be successful writing science fiction for young adults.

Horror. In horror fiction, teen protagonists are often compelled to confront dire supernatural forces. Horror may, like fantasy, include imaginary or mythical beasts such as vampires, werewolves, and assorted monsters. It may be based on a strange union between science and fantasy, of which the original was *Frankenstein*. It can feature horrific events such as nuclear winter or plagues. Although readers may expect to be frightened into nightmares, the coming-of-age theme still prevails.

Are you good at describing terrifying episodes? Does your mind spin dark disasters? Horror draws on archetypal fears even as it exaggerates and twists the normal and paranormal. It's a special skill, because if taken too far the story collapses, becoming laughable.

This subgenre is quite popular, so if you can create horror, you might end up screaming all the way to the bank.

Graphic novels. Bigger, better comic books are multiplying. Action/adventure stories with the added bonus of fantastic illustrations—wow! (And sometimes *pow*.) To gain a sense of what's involved in writing graphic novels, read them. You may be surprised by the variety and creativity you'll find.

Do you see frames in your mind and hear sound effects while writing? Do you have a gift for telling stories through dialogue with a bit of strategic narration thrown in? You don't have to be an illustrator to write graphic novels. If you come up with excellent text, a publisher will put you together with an artist. But if you have a flair for illustration, get started with sketches and dialogue boxes—and join the graphic wave of young adult literature.

Historical fiction. History provides rich opportunities to create teen protagonists. So much history has been lived by young adults through the ages, people who wanted to do—and did—new things with unknown outcomes. How many were sailors, soldiers, pioneers, brides, husbands, parents, slaves, indentured servants, artists, travelers?

Do you research history in your spare time, for fun? Do you find yourself hanging around older relatives, asking questions about what it was like to be a teenager growing up in a different era? When you think of stories, are they about people from World War II, early America, ancient Greece or Rome? Are you drawn to books about the Dark Ages, the pharaohs of old, feudal Japan? If so, let your imagination lead you further into those distant times and create a living, breathing tale peopled with teens who play important roles.

A great story, well-written, by an author who has done extensive research, makes an enthralling read. I'd like to go on record as saying that I believe historical fiction for young adults will be making a big comeback soon.

Magical realism. In stories of magical realism, the supernatural view is accepted as legitimate, and it's woven into the fabric of the story. Dreams, visions, or mythology interpret the meaning of physical events. Reality is depicted as the result of human perception rather than a set of physical laws that can be studied in a lab. In magical realism, one event can be experienced in completely different ways by two people with different views. For example, a suburban American teenager might view a mugging as a piece of bad luck arising from being in the wrong place at the wrong time. However, a *curandera* (female healer in the Hispanic tradition), could interpret the same mugging as something arranged by the teenager's spirit, a spirit urging the teen to look deeper and value life more.

Have you studied mythologies or cultural mysticism? Are you interested in the meaning of dreams? Do you like to ponder how differently two people will interpret the same episode? Do you seek visions to help you understand life? Magical realism could be your niche.

This subgenre is growing in popularity. If you'd like to read excellent examples of magical realism for young adults, I suggest the books of anthropologist Laura Resau, *What the Moon Saw*, and *Red Glass*.

Humor. Humor can be part of any novel, and it enhances any novel it's part of. We all need to laugh, right? Including teens. Many YA authors put humorous moments into their books with great success, combining laughs with poignant understanding of adolescent struggles.

As an actual subgenre within YA however, there are few books that can be classified as "humor" first and foremost—though this may be changing. (An example that puts humor front and center from beginning to end is Louise Rennison's novel, *Angus, Thongs, and Full Frontal Snogging* and its sequels.) Therefore, humorous books are usually paired with another subgenre, e.g., "YA, humorous contemporary" or "YA, humorous fantasy" or "YA, humorous romance."

Do your words hit readers' funny bones? Do people chuckle when they read your account of the date that went bad, the school assignment that failed, the private blog that went public? If so, keep smiling—and writing.

Mystery/detective. The young adult mystery/detective novel is leaner and less gory than some adult mysteries. And, of course, crimes and puzzling circumstances are solved by the teen protagonist coming of age. This subgenre requires excellent plotting skills. Red herrings, misdirection and intrigues abound, with interesting characters who showcase human motivations.

Are you an incorrigible sleuth who loves to read mysteries? A student of human nature? Do you enjoy subjects like forensic psychology? Do you have an idea for a teen investigator who could solve a series of clever crimes or unravel a delightfully tangled web of lies? There will always be room for more good mysteries.

Religious fiction. In this genre, coming-of-age in a particular faith is the central story, whether about sudden conversion or a slowly deepening relationship with a higher power. Story lines may include resurrecting one's faith after losing it during a period of trauma, learning to resist temptations toward violence or self-destruction, finding satisfaction in service to others, gaining compassion for someone who's been getting under a character's skin...the possibilities are many.

Maybe your own faith is so central to your life that you want to give it a central place in your fiction. Whether you attend a church, synagogue, temple, mosque, or shrine, you can write about what's meaningful to you. In fact, this genre is fast growing—especially the area of Christian faith.

Romance. First love, anyone?

Young people will walk through fire for each other. They will transform themselves from spoiled to selfless, from haughty to humble, from wimps to wonders. And stories of young adults falling in love take on added fascination when members of the pair come from divergent backgrounds or when parents disapprove.

Young couples struggle to be taken seriously, to get a grip on powerful emotions, to find the time or place to be together at all. Feeling so much for someone else can be consuming. What's the difference between love and infatuation? Does the relationship allow each person to feel more like himself or herself? Or does it ask individuals to lose sight of their own personhood? These and many other themes can be explored in a context of coming of age.

Do you keenly remember the feeling of first love? Do you create characters in your mind who whisper of intense emotion, sacrifice, and emerging from the tempering fires of passion? Love stories will be treasured forever and ever, so if romance calls to you, let yourself answer with head-over-heels enthusiasm.

Your book. Publishers like to know up front what genre they're looking at, so it makes sense to study the categories outlined above so that you can accurately designate your book's subgenre in a query letter. (See Chapter Five, "Submitting Your Manuscript.") You'll want to feel comfortable speaking about your "YA mystery" or "YA multicultural" novel. For a more in-depth understanding, consult your library and bookstore shelves. Your local teen librarian is also a great reference. Your best education lies in reading many titles from each category.

The type of book you write is important. Once you establish a following, those who love your work will seek out every novel you've written. And whereas some readers will cross freely from one subgenre to another and back again, many others will stick devotedly to their chosen preference, whether fantasy, sci-fi, multicultural literature, or something else.

YA Subtypes

Reviews of teen literature often designate the book as suitable for "readers 12+." Quite a range. A twelve year old is a long way from an eighteen year old. Both may enjoy the same book, but for different reasons.

Because of the broad range of readers, the young adult category has divisions within itself. Two subtypes in particular deserve mention.

Tween. Tween books are aimed at 10-12 year olds. The protagonist is usually 12-14. The primary audience for such books is late elementary and early middle school students. The coming-of-age theme still applies, but there may be less complexity in the characters and fewer subplots. The resolution is more apt to work out well for all concerned.

Examples of tween fiction include Claudia Mills's *Lizzie at Last*, Louis Sachar's *Holes*, Elise Leonard's *Al's World* series, and Mary Peace Finley's *Meadowlark*.

Crossover into adult. Sometimes a book finds a readership among as many adults as teens, even though the book's basic theme is coming-of-age and the protagonist is a teenager.

Crossover stories showcase deep human issues across a broad spectrum, issues such as awakening to one's inner self, confronting identity, the role of the individual in society, and the search for love and meaning. There are many such books, among them Orson Scott Card's *Ender's Game*, Laurie R. King's *The Beekeeper's Apprentice*, Sue Monk Kidd's *The Secret Life of Bees*, and Harper Lee's *To Kill a Mockingbird*.

What About Market Trends?

We've all witnessed the way a given subgenre can take off. For a couple of years fantasy might dominate the market. Then horror. Then something else. How do these market trends affect you? Should you consider them when writing your novel?

I've met a number of aspiring writers who have stopped writing about what truly interests them and taken up a substitute interest they think has more market appeal.

"Everyone wants to read about _____ so I'll write about _____ to be successful," they say.

Publishers sometimes unknowingly contribute to this problem by talking about what's hot and what's not:

"We're not publishing much historical fiction this year."

"We're looking for a great detective novel with a female protagonist."

"Fantasy is on the way out."

"What the teen market needs now is some good horror fiction."

"We won't consider books written from an omniscient viewpoint."

My opinion: Trends come and go, but your best work will always be your most authentic work, and your most authentic work will not be determined by market forces.

Wouldn't it be sad if your voice cried out to write a dazzling historical novel, but because you'd heard that such a book would never be published, you quashed the idea and wrote horror? Your horror fiction could easily be rejected as "not right for us at this time"—and a year later you might see historical fiction go leaping full force into the marketplace.

Far more satisfying to write the book you really want to write, and then wait for the market to change in your favor, than to put your time and effort into a "coattail" title that gets lost in the flurry of transient popularity within a different subgenre.

For example, I wrote *The Seer and the Sword* before Harry Potter became an international sensation. Back then, fantasy was thought to be, if not dead, in dire need of medical attention. When my agent was shopping my manuscript, *Harry Potter* was just coming to fame in Britain. *Harry's* success probably contributed to the sale of *The Seer and the Sword*, but I hadn't written my fantasy because of it. And now there's a glut of fantasy literature on the market, so the trend is ready to swing over to something else—such as historical fiction.

The market is ever changing. You can count on it. Ultimately, your greatest market appeal will come from writing something captivating and enlivening. You're bound to write in a more captivating, enlivening way if you write about what truly calls to you. Your secret heart knows what kinds of stories will inspire you to create a novel that pulses with life. Pay attention.

When writing a book, comparing yourself to others is not only unhelpful but misleading. Remember the Ugly Duckling? The poor "duckling" was reviled by his tribe, cast out and left to die, because he didn't look like other ducklings. Yet somehow he survived to grow up—only to discover he was really a glorious swan.

The duckling did not *turn into* a swan. He was a swan all along but didn't know it. Moral of the story? Know what sort of bird you are.

You're the best at being you. You'll be the best at telling the stories you have to tell.

If you're saying what you really want to say, the way you want to say it, chances are good you'll strike a chord in someone else. If you're *almost* saying what you want to say, not quite the way you want to say it, chances are excellent you'll write something that fails to resonate. And if you're saying what you think others want you to say, the way you think others want you to be saying it, your story will be missing an oh-so-important note.

It will be missing *you.*

Controversy in YA Literature

What if the teens in your novels use profanity? What if they have sex or get mixed up in violent situations? What then?

Chris Crutcher drew on his experience as a family therapist and child advocate to create books like *Staying Fat for Sarah Byrnes* and *Whale Talk*. Crutcher's fiction includes themes such as injustice, prejudice, and being a social outcast. His protagonists sometimes use profanity, just as many teens use profanity in real life. Crutcher doesn't pull any punches, but manages to write believably about the power of love and courage to overcome abandonment and abuse.

Patrick Jones is another YA writer who creates believable voices for teens struggling with harsh issues. Titles like *Nailed* and *Chasing Tail Lights* showcase evocative characters trying to grow up in difficult situations.

Attempts have been made to censor Chris Crutcher. On occasion, Patrick Jones has been "uninvited" to speak at schools when people realized what type of fiction he writes. Both authors refuse to pretend that today's teens live sealed away from profanity or violence. Firsthand experience tells them otherwise. The profanity and violence in their books is never gratuitous, though. It's there as a seamless part of the story.

Some of the gatekeepers of YA literature—parents, teachers, librarians—object to realistic fiction. Strenuously. If your books show young people using profanity, having sex, or experiencing abuse, be prepared for some fallout from gatekeepers, some of whom will believe your work belongs in the adult section.

On the other hand, many gatekeepers for teens strongly support realistic YA, knowing troubled teens can identify with characters created by Crutcher, Jones, and other authors. Edgy books are finding more and more acceptance in the marketplace, too.

Though I read realistic contemporary YA, I don't write it, so I'm not an expert about it in the way Crutcher and Jones are experts. But I do know that no matter what you're writing, if you water down your voice, you dilute your story.

To write a compelling novel, the story must always come first. I vote for giving yourself permission to write the very best novel you have in you, whatever it's about. Sometimes the best books for teens allow the raw truth of a writer's innermost heart to bleed onto the pages.

CHAPTER TWO

FINDING *your* WRITING SELF

FINDING *your* WRITING SELF

BETTER TO WRITE FOR YOURSELF AND HAVE NO PUBLIC,
THAN TO WRITE FOR THE PUBLIC AND HAVE NO SELF.
– CYRIL CONNOLLY

Remember the first author whose words reached across the page, holding you so tightly you couldn't stop reading and never wanted the book to end?

Astonishing! And then it happened again, with another book by a different author, a book written in a different style.

Discovering variety of style in books is as delightful as finding new foods in restaurants. Some novels urge us to gobble them like crunchy chips at a teen party. Some we munch through steadily, like healthy sandwiches after an invigorating hike. And others seem to call for small bites, like chocolate mousse. Now and again, we'll even come across words we want to spit out—words too bitter, pungent, or sweet for our taste.

Literary sensations are cooked up daily by hundreds of authors of YA novels. To take your place at the YA table, it's essential to bring out new flavor combinations—which is what this chapter is all about.

Your Writing Self

There's an important "you factor" in writing. It's why you care to create a story in the first place, what you bring to your writing from your life and times, the types of scenarios you invent for your characters, and the way you go about the work of writing itself. It also ties in to your choice of subgenres, because some will fit you and some won't.

For instance, I'm often asked, "Why do you write fantasy?"

The honest answer: "Because that's where my mind tends to go."

Why do I have such a big interest in alternate realities and qualities of spirit? My upbringing surely doesn't account for it, unless I was rebelling against it. My dad was a physicist and an engineer who guided rockets to the moon, an atheist who taught his children that science alone defined what was real. When I was twelve and asked my mom what happens when people die, she answered, "Back to the carbon cycle." (She has since changed her views.)

Yet from the time I can remember, I made up stories about imaginary lands. I liked to ponder the nature of the soul. Like many children, I also saw things in my room at night, things that weren't there. My parents would sigh and repeat their mantra: "It's just your imagination."

Because I was good with words, my dad thought I should go into law. He also tried very hard to get me to be more practical. I once attempted to explain how, for me, it was impractical to be practical. Then he *really* thought I'd make a good attorney.

Could I have made it through law school? Probably. Would it have been appropriate to who I am? No way. Might I, like my little brother, have attained a PhD in chemistry? Most likely. Then maybe I could have written a science fiction novel about a misplaced beaker, the crucible for an important formula. Hmmm, well, interesting as that sounds...No, thanks.

According to the beliefs surrounding me as a child, fantasy was just plain invalid, a distraction from the life I was supposed to lead. For a long time, I had a big fear of being exposed as a dreamer spinning otherworldly tales. Heavens! What folly. But I got over that—even got to the point of saying, "I don't care if anyone reads my books but me. I still want to write them."

I doubt I'm unusual in feeling that my upbringing ran counter to the writing voice I eventually discovered. The thing is, we're not writing to please our parents, our siblings, our in-laws, pastors, teachers, bosses, friends. They aren't relevant to the process of creation, except insofar as they live deep within us—in which case, they're so much a part of us, we'll express them without working at it. Naturally. Yes, your writing may surprise friends and relations. It could shock your boss. Might not meet with your cat's approval.

Write anyway.

As you do, go for the strength of authenticity. Undiluted. Perhaps nowhere is this more important than in novels for young adults, where readers are hungry for strong, original voices.

How do you develop your own strong, original style? How do you recognize and develop your unique "writing self"? In my workshops, I have found the following exercises to be very effective at helping writers and would-be writers gain more access to their creative minds, the source of their originality. The exercises also help participants "get at" the YA material they have inside them.

I invite you to participate in the exercises to whatever degree you find them useful. Some will speak loudly to you. Others might not even whisper. Just do whatever you feel drawn to do.

The exercises approach the creative mind from several directions. All approaches are meant to lead to a similar place—the place where your own creativity takes over.

Writing Exercise

Animal, stone, plant

1. Find a place where you can relax and write. If you normally write on paper, use a blank sheet for your starting visualization. If you usually write with a keyboard, imagine a blank screen.

   Close your eyes and imagine the blank sheet of paper or document screen. Then imagine an animal appearing in the space. (Don't question what you see, just go with it. If you don't visualize easily, that's all right, just let yourself hear the name of an animal or feel its presence.)

   Now interview yourself about this animal, and write down your answers. What animal is it? What is it doing? What are its surroundings? What do you know about this animal? What does it symbolize? What are its most likable qualities? What's scary about it? Is there something about this animal that makes you uneasy?

   Write down everything you can think of about this creature. Then research it. Gather facts and lore about it. Make notes.

2. Go back to the first step, but this time, substitute a stone appearing in the space. (There are no greater or lesser stones in this exercise. Please don't judge your stone, which would defeat the purpose.)

What stone is it? What does it look like? Where is it? What do you know about this stone? What does it symbolize? What do you like about it? Is there anything about it that makes you uneasy?

Research your stone. What facts and lore do you discover?

3. And now, use the same process, but this time ask that a plant appear.

    What plant is it? What does it look like? Where is it? What do you know about this plant? What does it symbolize? What do you like about it? Is there anything about it that makes you uneasy?

    Research your plant. What facts and lore do you discover?

4. Now, imagine a situation where all three—the animal, the stone, and the plant, are grouped together. Don't worry if it doesn't make sense to you: just let the grouping be whatever your mind shows you. Make notes.

5. Your animal, stone, and plant are symbols given to you by your own creative mind, a mind that knows you very well. Now, pretend your animal, stone, and plant have messages for you. Ask yourself the following questions:

    What does my animal have to tell me about my writing self?

    What does my stone have to tell me?

    What does my plant have to tell me?

    Imagine the animal, stone, and plant are speaking directly to you, or writing to you. Allow yourself to feel and express anything that comes to mind. Don't worry about whether any of it makes sense immediately. It's just an imaginative exercise, but maybe you'll learn something important about yourself and the writing that suits you.

    When you have finished gathering images and messages, ask yourself what, overall, your creative mind seems to want you to know. Let that understanding flow into words.

Examples. To illustrate, here is a summary of one writer's responses to the exercise. We'll call her Carla.

Carla sees a coyote running in a vast, fenced field. She knows that a coyote is an adaptable animal with a scary, howling voice. She isn't sure what it symbolizes, but she is afraid of its howl. As a child, she used to hear coyotes howling, and they frightened her. She is uneasy because the coyote is fenced in when it should roam free.

When she researches the coyote, she finds out the following:

Coyotes live in pairs. They're diurnal. They can run over 40 mph. They can jump four yards in one leap. Sometimes they hunt alone and sometimes in packs. They are native to western North America. They are omnivorous, eating everything from rodents to vegetation to garbage. They came under violent attack in the second half of the 20th century, so much so that 20 million of them were killed. Still, they have managed to increase their numbers because they're so adaptable and intelligent.

Coyotes appear in many Native American myths and legends, wearing the face of the mischievous trickster and the hero. They usually play roles involving humor and cleverness.

In the stone part of the exercise, Carla sees a big, polished, shining diamond that is "pretty and sparkly." She thinks it symbolizes eternity. She likes that it is attractive and fun to look at. She is uneasy because of the controversy surrounding diamond mining practices.

When she researches diamonds, she finds out the following:

Diamonds are the hardest natural substance in the world. They're extremely valuable. Because they're so hard, they're used in industry as well as jewelry. They can cut through bone and rocks. They conduct electricity.

Diamonds have to be cut and polished by other diamonds, and this can only be done by very precise methods. Despite its hardness, if a diamond is hit in just the right way, it can shatter.

In the plant part of the exercise, Carla sees a tall saguaro cactus with three branches, sitting in the desert under the moon. She doesn't know much about saguaros—only that they save water. She isn't sure what the cactus symbolizes, but she knows it is a survivor. She doesn't like that it is covered in prickles.

When she researches the saguaro, she finds out the following:

The saguaro is a really big, long-lived cactus. It grows slowly—about an inch a year—but it can get to be 50 feet tall. It's so good at storing water that it flowers every year no matter how little rain it gets. White flowers. It has red fruit that desert creatures love to eat. This fruit used to be an important food source to some Native Americans; each piece has thousands of seeds. Saguaro wine is made from the juice. Woodpeckers and flickers make holes in the trunks of saguaros and then live in them.

When Carla imagines the coyote, the diamond, and the saguaro grouped together, she says, "I see the saguaro hung with diamonds like a Christmas tree covered with ornaments. The coyote is sitting in front of the cactus, smiling up at the diamonds."

The messages? She feels that the coyote is telling her that her field is vast. The stone is telling her to let herself shine. The saguaro is pointing out that solitude and conserving her resources are very important to her.

Here's how she analyzes what the exercise tells her about her writing self:

It's surprising, but I feel happy every time I think of the image of the cactus hung with diamonds and the coyote smiling up at them.

I recognize there's a certain sharp edge to the things I enjoy writing, an edge that's sometimes controversial. Like a diamond. And I'm obsessively precise with every word, trying to polish to perfection. I also always incorporate humor into my writing, like the laughing coyote. The cactus image reminds me that I feel protective of my solitude when I want to write. And I'm prickly about criticism—if it comes too soon in the writing process, I give up even if I know what I've written is good.

The saguaro in the center of the group seems to be emphasizing how much I need solitude and contemplation to write. When I get enough of it, I can be prolific, like the saguaro seeds. I can go a long way on very little—a cactus flowering without rain.

When I think about the coyote's scary howls, I realize I've been afraid of coming on too strong with my voice and scaring people off. Maybe it's time to get over that. No surprise that the coyote is running—I'm always running. But I've fenced myself in, and that's not necessary. I'm in the middle of a vast field. I can try different types of writing and just have fun with it, loping along beneath the moon.

Another writer, Suzanne, sees a grasshopper, a garnet, and a yucca. She researches all three, and analyzes what the exercise has to say about her writing self:

The story I found about the grasshopper and ant resonated because I keep getting distracted from writing, always feeling there's something I "should" be doing—and writing seems like an indulgence. I feel a sense of relief knowing that when I'm writing I do better if I stop planning/thinking/working and just be spontaneous, like the grasshopper. I think the grasshopper is telling me to make the leap.

The garnet reminded me that I want to write about the dark side, outcasts, horror mysteries, things like that. It's time to make a commitment!

Finding out how the yucca has a specialized pollinator really got me thinking. I realized I need to get serious about having my own laptop because the way things are set up now my husband and I have communal computers in the living area. This doesn't do much for my "pollination." And igniting at a low temperature is so true of me—when I'm on fire, I like to write fast, and feel like I've simply got to get it down right away. Without a laptop of my own, I don't make use of the moment.

Delving deeper. Try opening up a dialogue between your animal, stone, and plant. This could be particularly helpful if there are obvious difficulties in your grouping of the three. For example, a participant in one of my workshops found that when he put the animal, stone and plant together, he saw the stone striking the animal, badly hurting it. Another participant found his plant strangling his animal. In these cases, letting the symbols "talk things out" can reveal valuable information about your writing self.

Writing EXERCISE

Meeting yourself. This next exercise is about recognizing things that may help you write, things hiding in plain sight. It's based on the idea that there's a human tendency to underrate our own experiences, thinking anything *we* can do must be commonplace.

Get into a relaxed setting where you can write. Put your name at the top of the page. Underneath your name write, "Assignment: Write a Novel for Young Adults."

Then close your eyes and imagine you are not yourself but rather an interdimensional traveler who has just landed in the life of the person whose name appears at the top of the page. In this exercise, you—the traveler—have been given the assignment of getting this person to write a novel, and now you're going to take inventory of what you have to work with. You'll be able to look through everything in the person's mind, heart, skills base, experience—anything that might help your mission.

As the traveler, begin writing down what you discover about the person whose name is at the top of the page.

First make notes on qualities of mind and heart. What sort of mind does the person possess? Creative? Persistent? Flexible? Inventive? Courageous? Curious? Write everything down, even traits that seem problematic, such as *undisciplined*, *stubborn*, or *timid*.

Now jot down skills this person has, and experiences lived. All of them. As an interdimensional traveler, you never throw anything away. Nothing is ordinary or useless. Feeding pigs is as valuable as rubbing elbows with executives; making snacks for toddlers ranks evenly with performing neurosurgery.

Next, write things the person has always dreamed of doing—perhaps skydiving, basket weaving, or sword juggling. And what does the person wish to know? A new language, geology, how to interpret dreams?

Based on your notes, what sort of author do you suppose this person will be? How will his/her character traits, skills, interests and experiences come together in a writing voice?

As you do this exercise, really consider the person at the top of the page as if you were meeting for the first time. Let yourself be amazed and interested, with the fresh perspective of an inquisitive traveler, a traveler with the mission to turn you into a novelist.

Using What You Know to Create Characters

Teen readers—and adult readers of teen books—love the feeling of finding fictional characters they can relate to, characters who get under their skin, characters they wish they could meet.

So where do those characters come from?

Everyone you've ever met has given you material for character creation. You observe traits wherever you go and whatever you're doing. Then you mix them up, exaggerate them, distort or reinvent them to create characters with personalities of their own.

Observation is key to feeding your creative mind what it needs to make memorable characters. But I think it's equally important to let go of any formulaic notions when it comes to creating those characters. Fictional beings are not assembled piece by piece from individual traits—they're not like lawn mowers or smoke alarms. At some point it becomes time to simply allow your creative mind to get to work and make up a whole person.

To put it another way: This ain't no thinking thing. I don't know exactly how fictional characters come to life. But they do. And they're more likely to be worth knowing if we writers take our greasy, analytical fingers off the process of their genesis.

Suspend analysis. (Don't ask what Freud or Jung would say.) I learned a long time ago that analyzing my characters could kill them off more effectively than any stabbing. They might continue to stumble around, zombie-like, for a while, but eventually it became all too obvious they weren't alive.

Maybe I shouldn't speak for all writers. Maybe some assemble characters like they would put together a lawn mower, trait by trait screwed into place. But when I'm writing fiction I fling my mechanical brain into the biggest abyss I can find and then humbly beg my creative mind to handle the task of character creation. That way, the characters seem to live and move and have their being apart from me. Which makes them easier to write about. (Again, don't ask what Freud or his buddies would say.)

Writing
Exercise

Your inner teen. When writing YA books, you obviously want to create characters who will appeal to your readership. Getting to know your adolescent self again can be a valuable touchstone. You want that inner teen by your side as you write your book. He or she will help you more than anyone else.

The following list of questions is designed to invoke the emotions of teenhood. I suggest making notes to yourself as you go through the list. You might be surprised at which questions strike you more than others. Don't be concerned if the answers to some of the questions happened during times in your life that fell before or after ages thirteen to nineteen. Remember, the spirit of youth can move us at any time of life. The important thing is to get a feeling for how that spirit has affected you personally.

- What is your clearest memory of feeling alienated? Misunderstood? Betrayed?
- What is the most unfair thing that has happened to you? What did you do?
- In what way did your upbringing seem utterly different from that of your peers?
- When have you gone against peer pressure to follow your conscience?
- How do you react to authority? What's an example of authority being wrong? Right?
- What has been your moment of greatest rebellion? How about your greatest dream of rebellion?
- What's the greatest risk you've taken? How did it work out?
- Have you done something impulsive that had a long-lasting affect on your life?
- Have you been disbelieved when you were telling the truth? Have you feared the truth enough to lie? Or has someone lied to you about something important?
- What is the most traumatic historical event you have lived through? How close were you to the actual events of that history?
- Have you grown apart from a dear friend? If so, was it gradual or sudden?
- Have you ever been so embarrassed you wanted to sink through the floor?
- What's the most unconventional thing you've done? The most thoughtless?
- What's the biggest mistake you've ever made?
- Have you been in a situation from which there seemed to be no way out? What did you do?
- When was the loneliest time in your life? How did you deal with it?
- When did you first fall in love? What happened?
- Has someone important to you rejected you?
- Have you ever lost control completely or done something so wild you surprised yourself?

- Have you laughed so hard you cried? Cried so hard you laughed?
- Have you ever suddenly changed your appearance dramatically?
- What has been your most euphoric moment? How did it change you?
- What have you longed to do but never done?
- What have you yearned to find but never found?
- What and whom would you die for?

Teen voice. Now that you've finished answering the above questions for yourself, what sort of mood has been invoked? Do you have a sense of a teen voice inside you with something to say? If so, without stopping to analyze, write a paragraph or two in that voice.

If you have a YA manuscript you've been working on, let your inner teen scrutinize what you've written and give you suggestions for strengthening the characters.

Using What You Know to Create Conflict

Every teen who has navigated through adolescence into adulthood has known days when conflict seemed overpowering.

Yay!

What?

Well, stories need conflict—like a car needs an engine. When's the last time you were riveted by a book about a sweet guy who met a darling girl and everything went wonderfully well for them and then got even smoother?

YA fiction doesn't sit around. It flies down the road at high speed and then hits a major bump. For this pace, you need plenty of fuel.

You are about to be grateful for every adversity, challenge or hardship you've ever faced. The worst things in your life are now the best things, because they're going to grant you the conflict you need to fuel your fiction. Every bit of conflict will help you—not only your own, but also what you've observed in other people, and the troubles you've been told.

Writing
EXERCISE

Finding conflict. Use a notebook or computer to complete the following:

1. Write something you've wanted to say but never said. Don't hold back—this is for you and you alone. No one else will see it.
2. Describe a character who could and would say out loud what you've written. As above, don't hold back. Please don't go on until you've finished.
3. Now look at what you've written. Ask yourself in what way(s) you held back.
4. For whom did you hold back? Do you know why?
5. What does this tell you about conflicts you could make use of as you write?
6. Do the exercise again, but don't hold back. Go wild. Give yourself some attitude.
7. If you have a YA manuscript you're working on, take that attitude and use it to add believable conflict to your scenes.

Example. Any conflict you feel can be used to energize your fiction. I once discovered that I was holding back to keep from offending various bosses who still lived in my head.

I've held a bunch of different jobs, from baking bread to hosting radio shows. I've waited tables, painted houses, and taught anatomy. Those jobs allowed me to meet wildly different people—which is a great opportunity for a fiction writer. (However, at the time I held those jobs I didn't actually understand that I was training to be a novelist.)

I even worked in the corporate world for a while, and got exposed to many administrators/managers. Some were awfully rigid in their outlook (or so I thought), and it took many hours of frustrated pondering to begin to understand their motives. I really disliked working in situations where people seemed to be promoted because they were sticklers for rules or narrowly focused on the bottom line.

Later, when my corporate stint was over, I wrote *The Healer's Keep* and exploited the conflict I had felt about corporations by exaggerating and rearranging some of the more obnoxious motives displayed in those previous work environments. My mind came up with a class of characters known as "dradens" for the book. Duty-bound to enforce rules, dradens are thoroughly inflexible. Their infuriating ways add an interesting twist to my fiction, and make me appreciate all those days I wanted to slam my head in a file cabinet.

The teen protagonists in *The Healer's Keep* are naturally very much at odds with the dradens they encounter.

Process note: It was only after creating dradens that I realized their origins. And some characters never tell me where they come from. That's the creative mind at work. But I find that if I do exercises like the one above and pull up conflict, I supply my mind with material. Who knows—it might even be therapeutic.

Jot down a few ideas you have for stories. Look at the element of conflict in each. Which idea is the most compelling? Which conflict is the most gripping? See the relationship?

Taking a Look at Voice and Style

In finding out more about your writing self, it can be helpful to look closely at the works of other writers. Several of the authors interviewed in *Wild Ink* have contributed original pieces of writing to illustrate voice. Their excerpts appear here. (For longer pieces from these authors, read their published books, which are listed beside their names in the interview section.)

The first five excerpts below range through five genres: fantasy, historical fiction, realistic contemporary, humorous contemporary, and magical realism. As you read through the excerpts, put your focus on each writer's individual style. Notice how they differ.

- Contributed by Dia Calhoun:

    On Saturday afternoon, her half day off, Phoenix untied the smaller boat and rowed across Majesty Bay for the first time since she had been caught by the Kingdom of Darkness. In spite of the potion, Phoenix still felt a little sad, a little bleak, slightly battered like the oars she gripped. But the sky shouted its blueness, its gladness, a trumpet for the clouds making white chains to the west; and her heart lifted as the wind blew against her face.

How she had missed being out on the water. Her fishing pole stayed in the bottom of the boat. Today she was content just to row, to listen to the oars creaking in the oarlocks and to the water splashing against the boat.

A five-masted ship passed to starboard, its scarlet sails as full as the belly of a woman with child. A moment later, a pinnace skimmed by to port; its sails shone blue. Phoenix watched. If she had a ship of her own, what color sails would she choose? Blue? Red? Yellow? Or white as a gull's wing?

Phoenix was rowing far out near the mouth of the bay, farther than she usually went, when suddenly, all around her, luminous white bubbles frothed on the surface of the sea. They shimmered, arching, then swirled into whirlpools. Phoenix had never seen anything like it. She reached out and scooped up a handful of the white bubbles, then let them trickle through her fingers.

- Excerpt: *Dancing In Combat Boots*, contributed by Teresa R. Funke:

May 20, 1942, Auburn, Washington (journal entry)

Now I must decide what to pack. We're allowed only what we can carry, but no one has told me how to fit my whole life into two small suitcases. This morning we burned everything Oriental and some of our important papers. We lent our piano to one neighbor, our typewriter and china to another. Since we don't know where we're going or when we'll be back, it felt as if we were giving them away. They all promised to return our things when we come home, but we'll see. These people were once our friends, even after Pearl Harbor, even after the curfew was instituted for us. Now they're reluctant to talk to us, even to say good-bye. Funny they can't see that the war has not changed us, but them.

I'd almost forgotten I had this journal. I've never been much of a writer. I found it while going through my things just now. It was a gift from my teacher when I graduated from high school. Auntie says I shouldn't take it, that it might be dangerous, but my teacher once told us that writing frees the soul from the walls we build around it. If that is so, I may need this book where I'm going.

- Contributed by Patrick Jones:

  "Just because I'm in a cage, you don't have to treat me like an animal."
  The guard at the Genesee County Juvenile Facility doesn't respond. He just
  cinches the silver handcuffs tighter around my wrists.

  "Move along," he grunts through a pair of pissed off pursed up lips. I
  don't know this guy, but I recognize that look. I see that look a lot on
  Mom's face anymore.

  This is my first time in jail, but not my first time at a correctional facility. I'd been to Jackson Prison once to visit my father, but I won't make
  that mistake again. I'll make new mistakes.

  There's blood dripping down my forehead to the floor sounding like
  the tick tock of a clock at school. I spend more time watching clocks at
  Beecher High than I do paying attention except in Ms. J's history class.

  "It's not bad. It should heal fine," the guard says, pointing at the cut.

  I ignore his lie. Cuts don't heal; they callus. I look at the guard, then
  wonder why his first words weren't "What took you so long?" I do belong
  here, since I've been living in a cage of my own for seven years, ever since
  my little bro Harold died when I was ten. That's a lie too. He didn't die;
  my dad killed him.

- Contributed by David Lubar:

  Sept. 26th (journal entry from main character to his unborn baby brother)

  We had an assembly today. I guess it was supposed to inspire us. This
  guy did magic tricks and talked about how you can do anything you want if
  you set your mind to it. Everyone left the assembly inspired and uplifted. I
  learned to fly. Patrick built a cathedral. Kyle mastered Snohomish and
  Basque, two extraordinarily difficult languages.

  Before you get too impressed, I should point out that I was being sarcastic. Ms. Flutemeyer, my algebra teacher, uses sarcasm all the time. It's sort
  of like being beaten up with words. I sure hope she doesn't have any kids
  of her own. I can't imagine what life would be like for them.

  After you're born and you learn to use the dictionary, look up sarcoph-
  agus and sarcasm. They have the same root. Words are good, as long as
  they're used nicely.

Gotta go. Though it's hard to imagine I could think of anything more enjoyable than spending my free time conversing with a creature who currently resembles a shaved weasel. See—sarcasm.

- Contributed by Laura Resau:

The aunts explained that one by one we would crawl through the small doorway into the stone steam bath with Abuelita. Then they would put a wool blanket over the entrance. Inside, Abuelita would throw a cup of tea on the hot rocks, and spiral steam down over our bodies.

I peered through the little doorway into the darkness, at an orange glow in the back. This was it. Either I could stay on the same path as Sophie the Weak or I could venture out on a new path, give life a chance to happen.

I tore off my clothes, exposing my pale, blotchy body for only a few seconds before I crawled in and lay face down. Abuelita threw a cupful of tea on the rocks, and hot steam hissed up, pressing in on all sides. I pushed my cheek against the cool dirt and gasped for breath. She brushed a handful of fresh herbs over my back, my legs, my arms.

Two weeks earlier, I would have been paralyzed with fear, imagining my skin sizzling and peeling off like a roasted pepper's, the cilia in my lungs getting fried, my throat blistering and swelling shut. But now what I felt was something quivery new, fresh skin pushing through the old.

In the first example, Dia Calhoun writes in third person. Her rich, highly visual style reveals her character's emotional depth as she rows across strange waters.

In the second example, Teresa R. Funke, writing in first person, confides the thoughts and feelings of a young Japanese-American woman preparing to leave her home for an internment camp during World War II. (First person is unusually common in YA fiction, perhaps because it allows greater intimacy with a character.) Well-placed details about personal objects convince readers this narrator is in a lot of pain but trying to make the best of it.

In the third example, Patrick Jones draws us into a young man's first experience with jail. The narrator's reflections about his father, his mother, and himself are woven into descriptions of the guard. The young man's tone is a mixture of sadness, anger, and insight, his emotions boiling close to the surface.

Next, David Lubar gives us the humorous, biting voice of a teenage boy who is opening up in a journal, writing entries to his soon-to-be-born brother. Without ever saying so in words, Lubar's sarcastic, observant adolescent conveys his intention to love and protect his sibling, at the same time revealing a sense of isolation and inner rebellion.

Lastly, Laura Resau's first-person narrator, Sophie, describes the birth of a new identity during a teenage girl's experience of a native ritual. Resau's poetic yet matter-of-fact narrative style is beautifully believable, and her character's vulnerable honesty appeals to readers to shed their own dead skin.

Each author's style is quite different from the others as I'm sure you've noticed. Each tone is compelling, with a cohesion all its own.

But suppose Dia Calhoun tried to write like David Lubar? Or vice versa? What if Patrick Jones squashed his own style in favor of Teresa R. Funke's or Laura Resau's? The ingredients that make each writer special would be lost.

Here are two more writing excerpts from current authors. After each one, I've done my best to mangle the writer's style, thereby mangling the voice.

- Contributed by Denise Vega:

    If anyone had told me I'd be babysitting my boyfriend's boozed up mother on prom night while he was out with another girl, I would have personally tightened up her straightjacket before waving good-bye to her as she left for the loony bin.

    But here I was at Josh's house in my stunning "no one will see it now" three hundred dollar Jessica McClintock dress, making sure Blotto Mama was still breathing.

    She was, so I ordered a pizza. Even saints get hungry.

Now, the same story content, but rewritten in a bland style. What happens to the voice?

    I would have been upset if anyone had told me that on prom night I'd be watching over my boyfriend's mother after she'd had too much to drink. Josh went to the prom with another girl, leaving me to wear my new dress with no one to see it except his mother. I checked on her and then ordered a pizza.

- Contributed by Elise Leonard:

> The rest of our trip was much calmer. Except for the weather. It rained every day.
>
> Every...single...day!
>
> "I thought they call this the sunshine state?!" I said.
>
> "They do," Granny agreed.
>
> "And it's on every license plate," Keith noted.
>
> "So why isn't it sunny?" I shouted.
>
> I was getting sick of the rain. I was getting sick of being pruney. I would have complained, but really, how polite was it to complain about being pruney for the short term to people who were pruney forever?

Here's the same story content, rewritten in an overdone style. What happens to the voice?

> For the remainder of our journey, the weather was uncooperative for the most part. The skies opened up and pelted the streets unremittingly with heavy rain.
>
> "I thought this was the sunshine state," I shouted over the noise of swishing hubcaps.
>
> "It is," Granny answered, scowling into the rearview mirror.
>
> "It says so on the license plates," Keith pointed out.
>
> "Why isn't it sunny?" I murmured through clenched teeth.
>
> I decided complaining would be impolite, but the rain was getting into my head—a gray wet sogginess sullying my mood. I pitied the people who actually resided in this benighted environment.

Writing EXERCISES

Changing style. Your turn. Here are four more excerpts from YA writers. Try picking a couple of them to rewrite in a different style.

1. Contributed by Hilari Bell:

    "I can't believe you did something this dangerous, this irresponsible, without telling me," said Weasel, for perhaps the fourth time. "I could have helped!"

    "I know, I know, you always took me with you, when you did dangerous irresponsible things," Arisa supplied the next line for him. "But you tried not to. Anytime you did something dangerous, you tried to get rid of me!"

    The streets were emptier than usual at this relatively early hour—still short of midnight—but the rain kept most of the drunken roisterers inside. And it was always less frightening when you had company.

    "I gave you a choice," Weasel argued. "I said, 'This is going to be dangerous, but if you want—'"

    "No, you didn't. You said, 'This is dangerous. It's time for you to go home now.' I had to blackmail you into letting me help."

    "It wasn't blackmail," said Weasel. "It was persuasion. And at least I gave you a chance to persuade me!"

2. Contributed by Mary Peace Finley:

    I lift my arm from her shoulder. "Lenna, Mano wouldn't really hurt you, would he? I mean, your life isn't in danger, is it?"

    Her answer is an exaggerated rolling of her eyes. "He's my uncle! Sure, he'll be pissed off, but I can handle him."

    So much for seeing myself as some sort of knight in shining armor, rushing to her rescue.

    "I'm...I...I think...you'd better go to your hideout without me, Lenna." I pull the crinkled purple foil from the Dove chocolate out of my pocket and hold it in front of her. "Our first everything has to be right, but it can't be. Not yet." I let my fingers caress the line of her chin.

    With a deep sigh, Lenna slows Mano's pickup to a stop on the shoulder of the Gunbarrel. "Andy," she says, turning in her seat to face me, but then looks down at her hands.

    "I want you to know something."

    I unbuckle my seat belt and angle toward her.

"When it is right..." Her voice drops to a near whisper. "It may be the first time for you, and...I want you to know this. It...it will be the first good time for me."

3.   Contributed by Todd Mitchell:

Frank felt her standing behind him before he saw her. Instantly, the lunchroom grew quiet. He set down his milk carton and prayed that there wasn't a stupid milk mustache on his lip. Then he turned. Julie stood with the last note he'd written clutched in her fist.

"Is there a reason why you hate me?" she asked.

"What?" He could feel his cheeks starting to redden.

"Don't even try to claim that you didn't write this." Julie waved the note in front of him. "I saw your handwriting on your English homework. I know it was you."

Frank's heart sped as he realized that Julie had been interested enough in him to look at his English homework.

"Aren't you going to say anything?" she asked, scowling.

"I..." He wondered how he could possibly explain that he hadn't meant to hurt her feelings. That he meant everything nice he wrote, and he only said the mean stuff because Mark was taking credit for the secret notes.

"I can't believe you thought it was funny to send me fake notes," Julie said. She tossed the note at him and spun on her heel. "You're such a jerk."

"They weren't fake," he muttered, but it was too late. Julie had already stormed off, while students around him snickered.

4.   Excerpt from "Radio City," by James Van Pelt:

Mom took a heavy pair of scissors from the basin, then filled the basin from the bucket. Steam eddied off the surface. "There's a nurse in Australia who claims that putting children in casts is exactly the wrong thing to do." She snipped the scissors open and shut a few times. "Your muscles are paralyzed, but they're not dead, so we're going to remind them what it feels like to be active." As she talked, she worked her way down the cast, using both hands to clip through the plaster-stiffened cloth. Clarence wanted to shrink away from the blade as Mom cut past the knee and down the shin. "President Roosevelt himself recovered from polio, and look how far he's gotten. There." She pulled the cast apart like a long clam. Clarence's leg, marked with grime at the thigh and ankle, lay as pale as a fish in the middle. No mold! But it smelled like the root cellar. Clarence wrinkled his nose.

Mom moved to the next leg. When she finished cutting off the cast, she dipped a towel in the basin, then cupped her hand under his knee and gently lifted. A ripple of pain flashed from his knee to the back of his thigh. Clarence gasped.

"Sorry," said Mom. She draped the hot towel over his leg. Water pooled in the cast. "The Aussie nurse says that the muscles will respond to stimulation. I'm going to rub the muscles, but I also have to move your leg, son. It might be uncomfortable." She put one hand under his knee again and the other on the foot. Her serious eyes stared into his. Clarence nodded. Mom pressed the foot toward him while pulling the knee up.

Polio is the cruelest of diseases: it paralyzes but feeling remains. Liquid fire poured down his leg, like the skin would turn inside out. He scrunched his eyes tight. Thigh muscles stretched, moved, tore apart, melted, screamed a thousand tiny voices of death and torment, remade themselves into agony battalions, fought bloody battles, crushed each other with stones, ground salt into their wounds, flailed their backs with rose stems, broke their bones, pulled their fingernails off, stuck each other with rusty pitchforks, then twisted them deeper and deeper.

"There," said Mom. "That's one. Four more on this leg before we go to the next."

Getting Comfortable in our Writing Skin

Maybe it's possible to write fabulous books for young adults without revealing aspects of who you are that may have remained hidden before. But I doubt it. In my experience, if you're trying to conceal yourself as you write, the story will come out stilted and wooden.

You may be one of those fortunate people who don't think twice about letting the world see your inner mind. But for many of us, exposure can be daunting. I call it "taking off my mind" in front of my readers. Sometimes I feel a tad more exposed than I'd feel wearing a string bikini on a fashion runway (an experience I've mercifully been spared).

Speedos, anyone?

Somewhere along the way we get comfortable within our writing skin and develop our personal writing style, our voice. This can take a while, and anything that helps is worth doing. Invaluable.

Ever wonder why the word "voice" is applied to literary works? Well, when you think about it, a person's physical voice, whether used for speaking or singing, is so distinctive that a voice print of one individual cannot be duplicated by anyone else. There's something identifiably unique about it. And that same quality in written work—unique expression of self—is peculiarly irresistible to readers.

There's an intimate connection between the words you write and who you are. Keep exploring all the avenues of mind you care to venture down, your inner paths, your creative self.

Write on.

CHAPTER THREE

OBSTACLES *and* DEMONS

Obstacles *and* Demons

THERE IS NO TELLING HOW MANY MILES YOU WILL HAVE TO RUN
WHILE CHASING A DREAM.

– AUTHOR UNKNOWN

MOST PEOPLE NEVER RUN FAR ENOUGH ON THEIR FIRST WIND
TO FIND OUT THEY'VE GOT A SECOND.

– WILLIAM JAMES

The Lamppost

Late night, no moon, stars hidden by cloud cover, rain slashing down. A man on foot hurries home through dark streets, wishing he'd remembered to bring an umbrella. Businesses have closed. An outage has interrupted power to the streetlights. With his head down against driving wind, the man crashes straight into a lamppost. He stumbles back a few steps, rubs his eyes, turns and keeps walking. This time he bashes into the lamppost with his left shoulder. He staggers around, winds himself up and moves forward, only to run smack into the lamppost, hitting it with his right shoulder. Afraid and disoriented, he flings himself away, striking the lamppost with his back.

"Oh no," he laments. "I'm surrounded by demons!"

Obstacles

When writing a book from start to finish, writers often have close encounters with lampposts—and I'm not talking about the sort of lamppost found in Narnia.

This chapter examines some of the obstacles you may run into as you work to finish your book. If you have no trouble finishing, you won't need this section. But if you're anything like me or my writing buddies and you get stalled when a big heavy post seems to hit you upside the head, keep reading.

I know what it's like to wobble and wander and wend my way among unlit lampposts. I also know what it's like to finish a novel. And when all is said and done—or all written and done—there's nothing like the feeling of holding a book in your hand, knowing you've told the story you wanted to tell.

So how do you get from page one to the end? There's more to it than chugging away with a good idea. Often, you'll wrestle hefty demons—demons such as doubt, fear, and rejection.

I confess it took me a while to get past those demons. Not only do they have steel ribs, they also have faithful cheering sections, endlessly chanting.

Give me a D, give me an O, give me a U, B, T. What's that spell?

I still get surrounded. And I'd never claim to be graceful about the way I deal with doubt and fear when they are looming large. But it doesn't really matter whether I'm graceful or not, so long as I keep writing. And it doesn't matter if you're graceful, either. What's important is to move ahead.

Your dream. I'm going on the assumption that you dream of writing a book for young adults. Chances are you've had this dream for a while. If you're reading this chapter, your personal demons have probably knocked you off course more than once.

Maybe you've heard too many tales of overnight success, and you've talked yourself into doom and gloom, believing your dream is locked into a permanent blackout zone. It's easy to forget that the "overnight" part of a success story is hardly ever true. We don't hear how a dream is going until that dream is actualized. We don't receive reports on a triumph before it's accomplished. Only afterward.

Going for a dream involves uncomfortable quantities of risk. So much work must be done without any assurance from the future. But we all take plenty of risks every day, whether riding the light-rail to work, investing in real estate, or eating sushi. You might as well take some risks on behalf of the writing that matters to you.

Best writing advice. I'm about to give you the best writing advice I ever received. Interestingly enough, the advice came from a teenager.

I was writing *The Healer's Keep*. As usual, I was in the throes of doubt, wondering whether the book was the most frightful drivel ever conceived or had the potential, perhaps, to be a good read.

My daughter Rose, an avid reader, has never minced words. I knew I could count on her to tell me what she honestly thought, so I gave her the unfinished manuscript.

Rose was about fourteen at the time. She disappeared into her room for a couple of hours. When she came out, she went straight into the kitchen and started fixing herself a snack without saying anything to me. In fact, she was acting miffed. She handled the bread with more force than necessary and slammed the lever on the toaster with a loud clack.

Heart sinking, I asked, "Did you read my chapters?"

"Yeah," she said. Typical teenage brevity.

"So do you have any suggestions for me?"

"Yeah," she replied, reaching for the butter knife. "Finish it!"

Finish it. When Rose urged me to finish, I had one of those "ah-ha" moments. I realized not only that she'd liked the story well enough to be upset when it stopped midway, but also that she was giving me the best advice I'd ever receive.

Finish it!

I've come to believe that many of us go through periods when we'd rather keep the dream a dream than test ourselves against the pressures and obstacles that may arise bringing that dream into being. It can be easier to hope than to act. Easier to imagine a large book deal than face a rejection letter. Easier to daydream while doing dishes than invest the time needed to write down a story. But if we look closely at pressures and obstacles, we stand a better chance of getting past them.

Here's a list of some common obstacles (cleverly disguised as lampposts) that writers tend to stumble into.

Obstacle #1: Lack of Time

> HOW WE SPEND OUR DAYS IS, OF COURSE, HOW WE SPEND OUR LIVES.
>
> - ANNIE DILLARD

Lack of time seems to be the top complaint of people trying to complete a book. What takes away our time? Job, family, friends in crisis, health problems, community involvement, need for sleep, chores that have to be done, closets that need to be cleaned...

Fill in the blank.

Here's a true story about lack of time:

As a little girl I saw things in my room at night that weren't there. When I grew up, I'd still catch a glimpse of an imaginary being every once in a while.

When I was twenty-nine and pregnant with my second child, I was staying in a cabin in the mountains one night. I woke in the wee hours and sat bolt upright, thinking I heard someone breathing. I was supposed to be alone. As I wedged myself against the headboard and grabbed a pillow for protection, I saw a red-haired woman in a dark purple robe. She sat calmly in a chair at the foot of the bed, regarding me with quiet, knowing eyes.

I knew this wasn't a flesh-and-blood, here-and-now human, but a vision. The young woman caught me in her gaze and told me she was a seer with a story, a story about a prince who lost his father, his kingdom, his sword, and his freedom, and then rose to be the most famous warrior of his time.

And part of the future she saw was me writing her story.

She stayed a little longer, while I watched her. Then she vanished. Unable to go back to sleep, I jotted some notes before getting up to see the sunrise.

A month later Rose was born. I couldn't forget my vision of the seer, but I was much too busy to write about her and the prince she loved.

Years passed. I didn't get less busy. How many of us do? Parenting, activities, jobs, being a wife, moving a couple of times...I didn't have time to tackle a book about a seer.

Then came divorce. As a single parent with even more responsibilities, I had even less time.

But that's when I began writing *The Seer and the Sword.*

Eight years had whisked by since that night in the mountains. One day I said to myself, "I've had this dream long enough. It's time to do it or be done with it." I couldn't be done with it, so that meant I had to do it.

Never a morning person, I began to get up early to write before the day's routine began. Doing so messed with my biorhythms at first, but then I fell in love with the quiet magic of pre-dawn. The air itself seemed softer and more fertile, laden with imaginative possibility.

Do you ever think about psychic pollution? Maybe thoughts and worries and fears have a tiny electromagnetic charge. When I'm feeling down or at odds and have a chance to get out of town and to the mountains, my gloom tends to disappear. I believe it's because I've left the psychic pollution levels of the city behind. And in those early, pearly mornings of writing, I often felt that same clear-headed strength I feel in the mountains.

I also noticed that, in the morning, time had a quality like taffy. When my spirit was clenched in some way, time resembled hard taffy—unyielding and tough, seemingly impossible to work with. Yet when my spirit was open and light, time turned soft and malleable in my hands. It stretched a long way, much farther than I would have guessed it could, with flowing strands, flexible and sweet.

It took me five years to write my book. I didn't really know what I was doing, had to grope my way. I started and stopped many times but eventually finished. Revisions took another year. Now *The Seer and the Sword* is published around the world, from Japan to Argentina. The seer's prediction came true—but I had to do the work.

I know that your life and mine are different, but we're all issued twenty-four hours a day. Look for chinks in your schedule. When you find them, use a crowbar if you have to, but widen that crevice. Seize the opening. Write the book!

One usable page a day yields a 365-page book in a year. A hundred words a day (a couple of light paragraphs) yields a 75,000 word book in two years—a respectable length for a teen novel.

Maybe you, like me, do not churn out pages quickly. I used to think it was a fatal flaw to be slow. Then one day I looked at my garden. Different seeds sown on the same day germinate at different rates. But I don't berate the cucumber seeds or accuse them of being lazy if they're slower to grow than the carrots.

How long does it take to write 100 words? Well, naturally, it depends on you and what you're writing. But if you type 50 words per minute, that's only two minutes. Add in a lot of pondering and rewriting and throwing away. It's not unreasonable to say you could write 100 usable words in an hour.

It's all about finding your own pace within the schedule you have, and then making the most of it. Do you get time away from your job during lunch? Instead of going out, pack a sandwich and bring a notebook. Can't think creatively in the middle of your workday? Try getting up early to write when the day is fresh. If short bursts aren't your style, schedule a block of time during your weekend, evening, or morning. Do you watch TV or surf the Net? How many hours? Cut back, and watch your manuscript grow.

Every excuse looks valid until we hold it up to the light and realize it's a line of absurdity. So go ahead. Examine your excuses about time. Hold them up to the light, and they'll shrink like shadows.

Bonnie's story. Within minutes of meeting Bonnie Callison in her little bookstore called Train of Thought, I was laughing with her. I don't remember exactly why—something about the difference between a romance and a mystery. Soon we were fast friends.

Though normally poised and confident, Bonnie became timid and small voiced when talking about her aspiration to be an author. She'd never written more than a few chapters of the books she had in mind. Why? She didn't believe she had time.

Bonnie was an advocate for books, well-read with a master's degree in technical writing, but none of that helped her feel better about her ability to write the stories closest to her heart.

Finally I persuaded her to hand over the beginnings of a manuscript. I loved it. I encouraged her to write more.

Bonnie was half finished with a novel that showed great promise when she died of cancer at 51.

Accepting her death was really tough, and somehow the hardest part was knowing she would never finish her book. What would it have meant to her husband and son to know how her story ended? How many other people might have been touched by her words?

Even if your days are packed, life is short. The amount of time we have here is unpredictable.

Obstacle #2: Rejection

THE GIRL DOESN'T, IT SEEMS TO ME, HAVE A SPECIAL PERCEPTION
OR FEELING WHICH WOULD LIFT THAT BOOK ABOVE THE "CURIOSITY" LEVEL.

– FROM A REJECTION SLIP FOR *ANNE FRANK: DIARY OF A YOUNG GIRL*

THE LORD OF THE RINGS HAS BEEN READ BY MANY PEOPLE SINCE IT FINALLY APPEARED IN PRINT...SOME WHO HAVE READ THE BOOK, OR AT ANY RATE HAVE REVIEWED IT, HAVE FOUND IT BORING, ABSURD, OR CONTEMPTIBLE.

– J.R.R. TOLKIEN, 1966

I haven't come across anyone who deals really well with rejection. Rejection feels terrible. Knowing you're in good company is small consolation.

But, oh, the company you're in!

Dr. Suess's first book was rejected 28 times before being published. His books went on to sell over two hundred million copies. J.K. Rowling's first *Harry Potter* book was rejected 12 times. We all know the next chapter in that story. Jack London received more than 250 rejections before first getting published, and he was the J.K. Rowling of his time. Those are just a few of many examples.

Books are rejected for many reasons. They may be poorly written or lack marketability. The publisher may have recently signed a similar project. And tastes differ.

Oh, man, do they differ. But if you enjoy peanut butter cookies and your sister thinks peanut butter is disgusting in any form, you go right on eating your cookies, don't you? You don't let your sister's taste interfere with your enjoyment.

You probably remember the first time a friend raved about a book that left you shrugging your shoulders. Likewise, you might have a favorite story your friends say is Valium in print. But your contrasting opinions won't make either of you sob into a pillow. I presume.

Yet somehow, if something we've written fails to pass someone else's taste test, it's harder to accept. Fiasco! Defeat. Blood-curdling despair.

Take a deep breath. It's okay. I know, that's easier to say than to feel. But as one who has occasionally flung herself into the pit of despair over rejection, I recommend humor as a more effective way to cope. Try running a copy of your rejection letter through a paper shredder, creating confetti. Hold a party in your honor. Serve chocolate. Laugh it up. You're doing something right. At the very least, you can't get rejected if you're not putting yourself out there.

Some writers have used their rejection slips like wallpaper—which seems to me like pretty awful feng shui. Some make their rejection letters into paper airplanes and fly them into a fireplace. One way or another, we all find a way to deal.

How many rejections should you expect to receive? As many as you do. Sorry to be flippant, but unlike my fictional characters, I'm not a seer. The average number of rejections for published authors is supposedly ten, but I don't know where that figure comes from or how anyone could tabulate the numbers.

All in all, rejection is not, in and of itself, an accurate assessment of worth. Plenty of writers have felt the sting and persisted to build wonderful careers. So think of rejection as an initiation rite of sorts, an entrance requirement to the author's club.

And always remember—you're in good company.

Obstacle #3: Doubt and Fear

IMAGINATION IS MORE IMPORTANT THAN KNOWLEDGE.

– ALBERT EINSTEIN

Who has not felt squashed by self-doubt?

I don't know what form your self-doubt takes. For some, it's a vague paralysis that creeps over the mind. For others it may be articulated in nauseating detail. Whatever the form, self-doubt is usually a variation of "I can't do this," or "There's no point."

When doubt is besetting others, it looks spindly and small to me. I think, "Why would she listen to that?" or "Why doesn't he see what a good writer he is?"

But let doubt rise up in front of me, and it appears to be a buffed-out giant with steel ribs.

Where do all those doubts come from?

Well, feeling doubt while you're in the process of creating makes a peculiar kind of sense. After all, knowledge brings confidence, but creativity is all about touching the unknown. Knowledge asserts "what's so." Imagination, on the other hand, is "the act or power of forming mental images of what is not present; the act or power of creating new ideas." (Webster)

The act or power of creating. That sounds good.

Images of what is not present. A bit more iffy.

And it's within that iffy zone that we find opportunities to create. In that same zone, doubt thumps its chest and utters convincing challenges. It's the nature of the beast, I'm afraid.

Another true story:

When I was seventeen, I went to college in Santa Fe, New Mexico. I had lived the previous six years in humid Wisconsin, at sea level. Santa Fe sits at seven thousand feet, and the desert dust makes sunsets that fill the sky, not only in the west but around the compass.

Behind the college was a small mountain named Monte Sol. Part of the Sangre de Cristo range. Uninhabited.

I wasn't the only one dazzled by the New Mexico sunsets. A group of us decided it would be a great experience to see the sunset from the summit of Monte Sol. One bright afternoon, several classmates and I set out, climbing the steep makeshift trail to the top.

The sunset was even more resplendent than we'd imagined it would be—a glorious blend of red, orange, and gold. As the last rays grew dim, it suddenly occurred to us that after sunset, night falls! We still needed to get down the mountain. And not a flashlight among us.

In fading twilight, we found the dirt path. This was not Wisconsin dirt, which holds together well; this was dry, sandy dirt, which slips away, especially when the path is steep. We scrambled along, clutching at scrubby piñon trees, while night thickened. Soon we couldn't see the trail at all, couldn't see our own feet in the darkness.

After a long bumbling trek and many scratches and scrapes, we made it back to the college grounds.

To me, that journey up and down the mountain is analogous to what happens when undertaking something new. Imagination inspires us, and we act. It's easy, at the beginning, to be so struck by a glowing vision that the thought of darkness is forgotten. We begin boldly, climbing high on the strength of the vision. Then we encounter darkness, and stumble through it.

As artists, we wouldn't want to miss out on the darkness altogether, any more than we would want to skip the light of day. Louis Armstrong, child of poverty and prostitution, wrote "What a Wonderful World." He sang of the "bright blessed day." He also sang of "the dark, sacred night." Why did Armstrong call the dark sacred? Maybe he was referring to the way that heartache and hard times can deepen creative urges. Or maybe he was talking about the unknown.

That unknown is mysterious. It resists control, cannot be contained by formulae, refuses to be ruled. By its nature, it does not engender confidence. But it also bestows the sort of wisdom that guides our footsteps when knowledge cannot help.

Imagination isn't limited by what is present, leading the way instead to what is not. Now, when I'm confronted by a plot problem, I no longer try to "figure it out" according to what I know. What's missing is what I don't know. When I let that be so, my imagination goes into the unknown and provides a new perspective. The unknown is generous that way—generous and unlimited.

I don't have anything against knowledge. Bringing a flashlight along doesn't hurt, nor does having the skill to use one. But when knowledge hogs the whole mind, we run the risk of getting set in our ways, of never wanting to do new things.

When stumbling through darkness, unable to see, it's tempting to try to use knowledge when imagination is what's called for. It's especially tempting when the darkness is deep. At that point it's hard to believe that what we don't know yet will help us the most.

Anyone who takes excursions through the unknown is likely to encounter the uglies of doubt, fear, isolation, frustration, and more. Sometimes they rise up with great fervor and make things very difficult. This is natural, normal, and to be expected.

If I believed there was a formula to KO every demon, I'd give it to you. But I don't. It's unknown.

Obstacle #4: Meant To Be?

IT IS OUR CHOICES...THAT SHOW WHAT WE TRULY ARE,
FAR MORE THAN OUR ABILITIES.

– J.K. ROWLING

There's a lot of talk floating around about "fulfilling your dreams" and "following your path." Sometimes the implication seems to be that if you're following your path to fulfill your dreams, obstacles will melt. Or the whole experience will be so joyous, any drudgery will transform into bliss. Along those lines, I can't tell you how many times I've heard, "I was planning to write a book but I guess it wasn't meant to be."

When I hear the phrase "wasn't meant to be" spoken that way in the context of writing, I'm not sure how to translate what is being said.

If it's meant to be, will the book write itself?

It's not that I don't believe some things are meant to be. I've had profound and joyous experiences of feeling led to a particular person, place, job, book, insight, chain of events, etc. I deeply appreciate the unseen help. It's precious. But it's not a sign I should sit back and wait for things to happen.

Suppose we approached other things in our lives with the attitude that they'd get done "if it was meant to be." I don't know about you, but I would never do the dishes. Not ever. I'd only occasionally weed the garden. Wouldn't be inclined to lift a finger to pay the bills. Working out? Not a chance.

How many people do you know who will go that extra mile for their job and be amazingly patient with all the bumps in the road on the job—and then tell themselves a dream should just fall into place or it isn't meant to be?

Art does not have a special exemption from sweat. Images of writers as artists whose work flows effortlessly or not at all are false. Equally untrue is the idea that artists must live for a while in the gutter dressed in elegant black, and then when they've suffered enough, their difficulties magically resolve.

Wild stories.

If you were first starting out at a gym and someone told you, "Getting in shape is going to feel delightful from the get-go. Burning fat is going to be a blast every day," you'd probably know that was a lie. Certainly after soreness kicked in, you'd know—or when you were huffing and puffing while building up an oxygen debt.

Plumbing the depths of your adolescent self, coming up with a story that really hangs together, writing that exquisitely awful first draft, going over it all again and again—takes work. Intensive, sweaty work. It ain't easy!

So if you're struggling to get your book written, there's nothing inherently wrong with you. Go to it, sweat it out, huff and puff. Keep going till you reach The End.

Obstacle #5 : Waiting for Inspiration

IF YOU WAIT FOR INSPIRATION, YOU'RE NOT A WRITER, BUT A WAITER.

- ANONYMOUS

Every writer loves the days when inspiration thrums in the air, when the words are flowing like babbling brooks, when the pages of deathless prose are piling up.

I can count on one hand how many times those days have come along for me. And in each case, sad to say, by the next morning it became clear that what I'd written was in desperate need of revision.

Everyone's different. Maybe you're the sort of writer who can afford to wait until you feel wildly inspired before you get going. Me, I find it helpful to approach writing the way I approach exercise.

I exercise on a regular basis. It tends to go pretty well most of the time, a reliable mix of work and play. I like to get the blood moving. Admittedly, there are days when I get out there in my cross training shoes and feel as if I'm slogging through a giant tub of goo. Then again, occasionally endorphins find their way to every cell in my system. But whatever happens, I know I'm not going to quit.

The more often I exercise, the easier it is to exercise again. Therefore, I can depend on my body for energy when I need it, and if there are sudden, unexpected demands in my life, I have more reserves available to deal with them—reserves built up by regular exercise.

In a similar way, the more often I write, the easier it is to write again. It's a level of writing fitness, exercising my dream body.

Dream body? Imagine the dream inside you as a body—a body that's visible to your soul. When your dream body is neglected it gets out of shape—puny and flabby and the whole bit. Undernourished. Sometimes it might even seem to be dead. But it isn't, and if you start taking care of it, it will get stronger.

It wouldn't be smart to load up on the heaviest weights your first day in the gym. And you can't expect your dream body to lift your entire dream immediately. Give it time, attention, nourishment and exercise, so it gets stronger. The stronger it gets, the more energy it will give you—energy for inspiration.

As with any fitness program, there's a lot to be said for making yourself accountable when exercising your dream body. Set a few goals. Realistic goals. Start with a paragraph a day if you have to. Fifteen minutes. One sentence, badly written. Make a daily appointment with yourself. Then keep your appointment!

What if your life depended on it? From a certain light, it does.

What about being accountable to other people? I'm of the opinion that when a dream body is still weak, you might not want to talk about it much. You can lose energy by yakking; the energy you need for taking action can go right out of your mouth. Really! Every time you talk about a book that isn't written, you could be draining away more of the reserves you need in order to write it. And if you entrust your hopes to the wrong people, you'll end up fighting not only your own doubts but also the fears others foist on you.

When you set a time or clear a space to write, inspiration will feel invited. Like a dear friend, it will pay you a visit. Do your friends like to call first before coming over? Do you like to have coffee, tea, and muffins ready?

But what if you believed the sign of a true friend was to beat down your door at unexpected times and insist on barging in?

Treat inspiration like a friend and it will be a friend to you. Don't wait for it to beat down your door. You might wait a lifetime.

So there you have it—a list of lampposts you may bang into as you write your book. You may have encountered one or two—or all—of the above. My hope is that by naming and facing them, the lampposts lining your way will stop surrounding you and start shedding light to guide your direction.

CHAPTER FOUR

RESOURCES *for* WRITERS

RESOURCES *for* WRITERS

If you're an old hand at writing with lots of practice honing your craft, you may wish to skip around in this chapter for the pieces of information tailored to the YA genre. Most of the resources explained here will benefit less experienced writers more.

Getting Started

Once you've decided you're really going to finish the book you have in mind, it's simply a matter of writing it. Right?

Right.

Writing an entire novel can be quite daunting—especially the first one in a particular genre. Plenty of people start off with a bang only to discover that writing the book isn't as easy as it looks. Like building a house, cooking a gourmet meal from scratch, or playing an instrument, writing takes skill and practice.

Where to begin?

First things first. If you're lucky enough to have a story idea that haunts you, that's a great place to start. You wake up with characters whispering in your heart. You see flashes of scenes in your mind's eye. The world of your story is as real as your morning coffee. Your creative mind is begging you to write. And that haunting idea is what will carry you through, giving you stamina, drive, and grit when you need it.

Yes, your story idea is fundamentally important. But many writers wonder, "How do I know if my idea can sustain a whole book?"

The short answer: You don't—until you've written the whole book. Sorry, but that's the excruciating truth.

You don't know, and I can't tell you. However, we can explore some things that may be of help. I can at least steer you away from some common plot holes and point you toward excellent resources.

Common Problems

Two of the more common problems that arise in writing for teens involve writing about real events and trying too hard to "teach" readers something.

Telling about real events. If you plan to write a book of fiction based closely on actual events you've experienced, you're heading for tricky territory.

I know I just got through saying it's a good idea to delve into your own life and write about what's real to you. It *is* a good idea, but only if you stay within the rules of fiction—which means you've got to have clear tension/resolution, character arc, and plot lines. If the story you're telling has really happened, you may feel compelled to faithfully convey the true chain of events. If you do, you're unlikely to wind up with an effective plot line.

Can an exciting book emerge from a true story? Without a doubt. We've all read examples of blazing good fiction based on true life. However, large numbers of writers trip up on this issue. They make the mistake of thinking something is automatically interesting just because it really happened.

If you decide to use actual events for the foundation of your novel, pick your details with care. Leave out the parts that don't serve. Make full use of poetic license. The story must come first.

Also remember that, legally, you can get into trouble if you duplicate real people without their express permission.

Preaching. Another problem some writers have is talking down to their readers. A condescending or preachy style is a big turnoff—especially for teenagers.

As a group, teens are much maligned. "Teenager" has turned into a derogatory term, variously synonymous with troublesome, unruly, scatterbrained and even criminal. Teens don't want to encounter this unfair stereotype when they read. They want to be respected, not patronized or lectured.

Does this mean you should avoid having a message? Not at all. Themes are important to fiction. For example, in my books, characters wrestle with how to use their gifts ethically, how to find courage after losing everything, and how to be stronger than calamities. But the reader isn't hit over the head. Messages are embedded in the core of the story itself.

Let's say you have strong feelings about teens ruining their future health by snarfing junk food, guzzling soft drinks, and getting only enough exercise to make it from the fridge to the computer and back again. You write a book with a character whose main activities are centered around snacking, soda, and surfing the Net. Primary interactions with that character consist of well-meaning people warning him about consequences and other characters luring him into still more unhealthy habits. You write scenes of his ensuing battle with diabetes and end with obvious conclusions about how his lifestyle has resulted in disease.

Your motivation is to make a point and get your readers to change bad habits. But will the point be taken? I think not. Teens, like adults, don't like great big vitamin pills shoved down their throats.

For a better result, you could write about a teen with a driving ambition to design world-class gaming software. Night after night he works late on his dream project, falling behind in homework, propping himself up with caffeinated sugary drinks and fistfuls of French fries. After some dramatic setbacks, he enters and wins a major software contest, only to have his best ideas stolen by a rival. As he searches for the identity of the thief, he's having strange symptoms such as blurred vision and excessive fatigue. He ignores his failing health and keeps pushing. At a crucial moment, he slips into a coma. A friend rushes him to the hospital, where he's diagnosed with diabetes. He gets treatment, changes his habits, identifies the thief, and successfully wins back his credibility in software design.

In the first story, the message is screaming at the reader from page one. In the second story, the message is embedded for the reader to discover.

An example from a well-known book of fiction is J.K. Rowling's creation of Rita Skeeter, a journalist whose pen drips lies about Harry Potter. The embedded message: Don't believe everything you read.

Some people worry that unless teens are bludgeoned with a blatant message, they won't receive it. Not so. Young people grasp complex ideas with ease. They're perfectly capable of adding profound perspective to any discussion. And they're certainly able to pick up messages left in the background of a book.

Another way to talk down to readers is by backing away from conflict, dancing around it, or inserting pat resolutions. Teens are ready for a more complex approach. Don't cheat on the conflict.

Weak or undeveloped subplots won't cut it either. Teens enjoy following stories within the story. Fill your plot with twists, turns, and interesting secondary characters.

A related matter—don't write as if the only thing young people care about is dating, sports, clothes, and social status. You'll miss the mark. Teens—particularly teens who read novels—are far from shallow. Look at the success of books by Joan Bauer, T.A. Barron, David Lubar, Chris Crutcher, Jerry Spinelli, and many more. These authors write profound coming-of-age stories and have legions of readers.

Respect your readers and they'll respect you back.

When writing, I make it easy for myself by simply assuming my readers will be faster, smarter, better informed, more savvy, and in all ways more brilliant than I.

Improving Your Craft

Your creative mind is begging you to write. You've got a story haunting you. You're ready to go. You put words on a page, and then more words.

You read it over. But the words you've written aren't telling the story you want to tell. Instead of soaring like your imagination, your words seem lifeless, like birds afflicted with West Nile virus.

Now what?

It's time to learn more about the craft of writing.

No one expects a painter to magically understand how to mix colors or master brush strokes without study and practice. Actors and dancers don't hope to be great without ever taking a class in theater or movement. Musicians know they must put in years before their instrument can speak with eloquence. The same goes for writing.

Fortunately, there are many things that can help you write better. I hope the following list will save you time and trouble on your writing journey.

Books. Dozens and dozens of books are devoted to the art of writing and the business of publishing. I've read scads of them. Some stand out as truly exceptional. Here, for your review, is a list of my favorites. Some are celebrated classics. A few are relatively undiscovered gems I was lucky to stumble upon.

- *Keys to Great Writing,* by Stephen Wilbers (Writer's Digest Books, 2000)

  After reading *Keys to Great Writing,* I felt as if I'd received an education worth fifty thousand dollars, though I bought my copy for a mere twenty bucks at the Tattered Cover Book Store in Denver. From intro to appendix, this book lives up to its name. Author Stephen Wilbers, a Fulbright scholar, earned his Ph.D. from the University of Iowa. To me, the essence of his brilliance is his gift for distilling knowledge and making it accessible.

  In his introduction Wilbers states: "No matter how tempting it is for teachers of writing—me included—to try to make it seem easy, writing is a complicated, challenging endeavor." (Amen to that.) Then he reveals hundreds of ways to make that endeavor less complicated and more effective. Though written from the perspective of improving nonfiction, many of the principles Wilbers communicates can be applied to fiction writing of any kind, including fiction for teens. Using artistry and humor, Wilbers starts with basics and builds to fine points. The reader benefits not only from his extraordinary level of knowledge but also from his years as an award-winning educator teaching college students to write.

- *Get That Novel Written!* by Donna Levin (Writer's Digest Books, 1996)

  Donna Levin's wonderful manual for how to write a novel is properly subtitled *From Initial Idea to Final Edit.* Her comprehensive discussions about writing for adults can easily be translated to writing for teens.

  Levin's style is so full of verve and panache, she makes it fun to discover what it takes to write a novel. Even her chapter titles are enticing: e.g. "A Plot Should Not Be Where the Writer Is Buried."

  Before I read *Get That Novel Written,* I knew very little about the essential elements of fiction: characterization, dialogue, plot, subplot, secondary characters, point of view, etc. It was Levin who gave me the knowledge I needed to write my own first book.

- *On Writing,* by Stephen King (Scribner, 2000)

  Prolific and mega best-selling author Stephen King is well qualified to speak about being a writer. His "memoir of the craft" relates his life journey with compelling, relentless honesty. There's something about reading King's account of "racing my own self-doubt" to get his stories written that is strangely reassuring. He's Stephen King, *the* Stephen King, and yet he confesses that if his self-doubt wins, his story will never see daylight.

On Writing opens with King's autobiography, showing how he developed the voice made famous by books such as *Carrie* and *The Stand*, books read by countless teens. In the section called "Toolbox," King offers a fresh perspective on the subject of writing itself, his quirky voice inseparable from the points he makes.

King began his professional life as a grammar teacher. (Yes!) And his book makes it plain that he did not just fall into the role of writer. He worked at it. He, too, collected rejection slips once upon a time. He, too, has wrestled with the blank page and found it to be appallingly intimidating.

- *Bird by Bird*, by Anne Lamott (Anchor Books, 1994)

  Why do writers smile wide when *Bird by Bird* is mentioned? Probably because many writers of all genres have encountered people who assume the writing life is a glamorous existence taking dictation from a Muse, while Anne Lamott's book exposes the more laughable and ugly realities. "Almost all good writing begins with terrible first efforts," she says as she advocates writing "shitty first drafts."

  Lamott details trial upon trial and tribulation after tribulation, from rejection to writer's block to being subjected to withering criticism. Her hilarious, whimsical style strikes a tone that helps her readers want to keep going and write another draft. And that, after all, is what writers may need most.

- *The Elements of Style*, by William Strunk, Jr., and E.B. White (Longman Publishers, many editions)

  First published in 1959, *The Elements of Style* has been updated several times. It has earned its place as a classic advisor on composition and style. Written by the author of *Charlotte's Web*, E.B. White, and White's English professor, William Strunk, Jr., *Elements* is filled with sage directions. It's a slender little volume that can be read in short bursts; I find it fun to open it at random.

- *Grammatically Correct*, by Anne Stilman (Writer's Digest Books, 1997)

  Got grammar?

  Stilman's subtitle promises an "essential guide to punctuation, spelling, style, usage and grammar," and that's exactly what she delivers. Her superbly organized book allows readers easy access to grammatical know-how from subject and predicate to the diverse uses of the colon. An extensive index takes the hassle out of finding examples relevant to specific writing situations. Stilman explains grammatical terms and linguistic concepts with clarity and finesse. In a word: comprehensive!

- *Writer's Market* (Writer's Digest Books, new edition every year)

  Writer's Market defines format requirements, submission guidelines, and markets for writers. It gives the most current information available, thus sparing writers an enormous amount of tedious research. Every year a thick volume of information is collected and assembled into this book that lists how, where and in what form writers can sell their work. Enterprising writers can also buy a CD if they wish, which gives access to updates for a year. Updates become necessary because editors and agents change houses, guidelines shift, and publishers may go out of business or new ones may arise.

  Markets are divided into sections: literary agents, book publishers, consumer magazines, trade journals, contests and awards. Agents are listed alphabetically with contact info and guidelines. Book publishers appear alphabetically with information on the types of books that a particular press publishes and tips on what the editors look for. Magazines are arranged by category from A as in Animal to W as in Women. (Teen and Young Adult under T.) A long list of contests and awards is found at the end of the book.

  The book has more information than any single writer could ever make use of, but it's a fabulous way to stay connected with the field.

- *UnJournaling,* by Dawn DiPrince and Cheryl Miller Thurston (Cottonwood Press, 2006)

  This unusual book is filled with short writing prompts to jog your mind into the flow of writing. On days when it seems your author pipes have filled up with sludge, *UnJournaling* is a great tool for getting the gunk out. And who among us does not have gunky days?

  Even if you aren't feeling bogged down, it can be refreshing to open this friendly book and read something such as: "Write a short conversation that might take place between two people who are unlikely ever to meet. For example, you might have Brad Pitt talk to Benjamin Franklin or Hillary Clinton talk to King Tut. You might write a conversation between your third grade teacher and Orlando bloom, or Martha Stewart and the crazy guy at the end of your street who seems to be collecting old tires." See what I mean? Ungunked.

- *Seize the Story,* by Victoria Hanley (Cottonwood Press, 2008)

  I realize I'm blowing my own horn here, but I want you to know about my other book on writing, a handbook for teens who like to write. Although the book is designed and written for teens, the information may be useful to any fiction writer. It details many "secrets" about technique. A number of award winning authors of YA literature share advice about writing fiction. Many of them have also contributed writing samples that illustrate approaches to setting, dialogue, and characterization.

All these books, and others you'll discover yourself, can help you immensely. The right book at the right time is worth far more than its cover price. Once you buy it, you can refer to it whenever you like.

I'd suggest browsing www.writersdigestbookclub.com or subscribing to magazines such as *Writer's Digest* and *Poets and Writers*. If your budget is limited, make a trip to the library.

Writing classes. Most community learning centers, colleges, and universities offer classes in creative writing. If you're short on discipline, class assignments can motivate you to complete essays, short stories, or even longer projects.

We've all been to school, so I don't have to tell you there are life-changing, extraordinary teachers working alongside those who are lackluster or disinterested. Not every writer is a good teacher, so you may have to do a little digging to come up with a class that delivers cogent and helpful instruction. But if you find one, it can spur you on and accelerate your understanding of the writing craft.

Writers' conferences. Writers' conferences commonly include workshops on the writing craft, marketing your work, and staying inspired. The good ones include opportunities to get a critique on a page or two of your manuscript and make a pitch to a working editor or agent. Some of these conferences have well-regarded writing contests for unpublished writers.

I'm not an expert on conferences. I've attended them only as a speaker or workshop leader. As of this writing, few conferences cater to people who want to write for young adults. However, you can glean information about the adult markets and then apply what you learn to writing YA literature.

I suggest doing research to ascertain if a particular conference is worth the investment of your time and money. Choices abound. Conferences can be excellent opportunities to hear firsthand from industry hotshots. Many of the bigger, more credible conferences are attached to professional organizations.

And that brings us to our next topic.

Professional organizations.
Writers' organizations give you the opportunity to meet kindred spirits, learn more about writing and publishing, and just generally connect with the writing community. For example, the Society of Children's Book Writers and Illustrators (SCBWI) is an organization with a worldwide membership (See www.scbwi.org). Local chapters provide members with gatherings, classes, and support. When you join, you'll gain access to information about writing and publishing in the children's market, of which young adult fiction is a part.

There are also professional organizations dedicated to genres of adult fiction. Mystery Writers of America, Romance Writers of America, and Science Fiction and Fantasy Writers of America all have regional chapters. (To date, Young Adult Writers of America does not exist.) Depending on the YA subgenre you're interested in, you could gain a lot of knowledge and support from attending conferences sponsored by these organizations.

Groups spring up to serve writers within a particular region as well. In Colorado, where I live, there are organizations such as Colorado Authors' League, Rocky Mountain Fiction Writers, Northern Colorado Writers, and others. All offer classes and writing contests. MileHiCon is an annual conference for sci-fi and fantasy lovers held in Denver.

Try doing a search for writing organizations in your area. Test the waters by attending a class or two. Organizational support has been very helpful to some writers.

In addition, there are organizations devoted specifically to increasing literacy among teens. The Young Adult Library Services Association (YALSA) is the fastest growing group in the American Library Association (ALA)–and the ALA has a long history of connecting media specialists throughout the United States. The

International Reading Association (IRA) is another effective organization dedicated to literacy. Both YALSA and IRA have outreach programs directed at young adults themselves. ALAN (Assembly on Literature for Adolescents of the National Council of Teachers of English) links teachers who work with teens nationwide. Authors can join any or all of these organizations, and membership fees are reasonable.

Voice of Youth Advocates and *KLIATT* magazines focus on teens and literacy. Authors can subscribe.

Is it coincidence that these groups have such resounding acronyms? I can't say, but they're all viable routes to get information and find community.

Taking criticism. At what point do you show your writing to other people? That's a big question.

When I was writing my first novel, I didn't show it to anyone but my children, my husband, my sisters, and one friend. This runs counter to the advice you'll get from other sources who say that feedback from close family members and friends has no value.

In my case, feedback from people who were close to me personally, particularly my children, was of great value. Both my kids have a knack for spotting discrepancies and plot holes. They were the perfect teenagers to tell me what they thought.

Back then I didn't know about critique groups, and if I had known, I probably wouldn't have joined one. I still believe that if you show what you've written to the wrong person at the wrong time, you risk sending your artistic self into hiding. When sharing your writing with other people, you lay yourself open to their reactions. Some of those reactions will be kind. Some will be mean. Some will be helpful and others completely off base. The main point—once you put your writing out there, you can't take it back.

There's a delicacy to writing, especially at first. When you write a story, you're exposing your innermost thoughts and feelings—your view of life. This makes you vulnerable.

Sometimes not showing what you've written is the best way to strengthen the relationship between you and the writer within. You don't dig up an apple seed to see how it's growing. You let it germinate and send shoots into the air and light. You water it. You wait until it's a good strong sapling before you hang anything on its branches—and you don't get angry if the tree doesn't bear fruit immediately.

However, it's also true that no one can read his or her own work for the first time. Good readers who will spot plot holes, cardboard characters, or stilted dialogue can be immensely helpful. When you get criticism from people who know what they're talking about and also care about helping you, it's worth more than you could ever pay. So just as showing your writing to the wrong person at the wrong time can hurt you, showing the right person at the right time gives you a chance to grow much more than you could on your own.

My first rule when receiving criticism—consider the source. In my experience, there are three categories of critique: constructive, destructive, and useless.

Constructive criticism comes from knowledgeable people who want to help you write better. They look over what you've written and make suggestions that tighten the structure, streamline the flow, highlight the characters, and help the plot stay on track.

For example, when I was writing *The Light of the Oracle*, I met with my editor—a gifted Englishman—in a coffeehouse in New York City. He frowned at the brimming latte cups. "You've written two books here," he said, "and you need to separate them."

My first response was ultra-eloquent: "Uh." Followed by, "What?"

He continued. "There are too many elements. Why are you bringing in the characters from your other books?"

To which I replied with articulate persuasiveness: "But—"

He held up a hand. "I want you to think over what I'm saying carefully. Do you really need the characters from your other books?"

"Uh, I was trying to tie things together more. The books are supposed to be companions." (Companion books are not really sequels but they're related to each other and take place in the same world.)

He adjusted his bow tie and shook his head sagely. "You must keep in mind the story you're telling."

Well.

I took a deep, deep breath, and then inhaled even further to complete lung capacity. As I considered what he said, the book cut itself into a million puzzle pieces in my mind, and then all those pieces flew up in the air and came down in a new arrangement.

I blew out a breath and knew my editor was right.

It wasn't exactly easy to rewrite the entire thing. The "two books" could not be cut into neat halves and then submitted separately. Everything was interwoven. I had to start over, taking out what didn't belong. But in the end it was a better book, with a clear premise and characters who could stand alone.

Keep in mind that sometimes an excellent critique may be delivered bluntly. Just because the delivery is blunt doesn't mean your work is not respected or the one giving the critique has nothing valuable to offer. Some of the best advice I've received has seemed harsh at first.

When I first started submitting *The Seer and the Sword* it was rejected a couple of times. Then my son told me to take out the prologue.

"You don't need it. It's the worst part of the book," he said.

"But why?" I loved the prologue.

"I don't care about the characters yet," he said. "It doesn't matter to me that Bellandra is falling, because I don't know anything about it."

I listened to him, removed the prologue, submitted the book again, and it was accepted.

When you're ready for constructive criticism, you'll crave honest feedback like a marathon runner craves water. You'll seek out people with a knack for editing and beg them to tear your manuscript apart. You'll want to hear what's wrong with your story just as much as you want to hear what's right. After listening to forthright comments about flaws and weaknesses, your heart will overflow with gratitude. "That's so true. I can't wait to fix that chapter..."

Nothing will get you to improve your storytelling faster than meetings with people who can give right-on critiques. Even one such person is worth a big bag of emeralds.

But destructive criticism is something else again.

How do you spot destructive criticism? The critique will be expressed in generalities that give you nothing to work with, statements like "This is the worst thing I've ever read," or "You have nothing to say," or "What made you think you could write a story?"

When listening to criticism, look for useful specifics. "I like the way this begins, but in paragraph seven on page two, I started to lose interest. It seemed repetitive." Or "The part where Donovan ditches Cheronne is well written, but why does she forgive him so easily?" Or "This chapter starts out at a fast pace with Ava getting close to Kira's secret, but it starts to fizzle on page five when Thelonius just sits around." Or even: "This first chapter leaves me cold. I think the story really begins where you have the second chapter now."

Destructive criticism would say, "This is a bad story." Or "Cheronne's an idiot." Or "Thelonius? What a stupid name." Or "I hate the first chapter."

The best way to handle destructive criticism? I'm not sure, but deep slow breathing is a start. Remind yourself it's just one person's opinion. You don't have to listen.

If you can laugh, you're home free.

Something else that deserves mention: If you always react to criticism with knee-jerk defensiveness, that's a different problem. You may be responding to constructive criticism as if it were destructive. If you've received specific feedback, think it over before automatically rejecting it. Is it relevant to your story? If so, you've just been given a precious gift. But if you feel too hurt to consider the merits of the advice, you're not ready to be criticized. (You may want to go shopping for a rhinoceros hide, because you're going to need it in the writing business.)

It's perfectly all right to back off and wait until you're stronger. And it's always a good idea to be selective about whom you invite to criticize your work.

One more category of criticism is the "useless" variety—criticism from well-meaning people who don't know what they're talking about. Either everything will be generalized in a glaze of positive comments such as, "This is the best thing I've ever read," or the advice will come out of left field, making ridiculous objections like, "I don't think your characters should tell the truth because people don't like to hear the truth," or "I think you should take out the part where Samantha knocks on Kareem's door"—when actually that part is crucial to the story you're telling.

Useless criticism is maddening, confusing and well. . . useless. It misses the mark.

How do you know when you've received a useless critique? Your mind, heart and soul will feel disjointed. Imagine if J.R.R. Tolkien, author of *Lord of the Rings* had been told, "Your book is good except for the Hobbits. Why not just tell a normal story?" Or if someone gave Harper Lee, author of *To Kill A Mockingbird*, a critique saying, "You give children too much credit—you should write from the point of view of adults."

Sometimes useless comments are so biased in your favor it's like talking to a doting mother who says, "What zit? I don't see any zits on your face," when it's obvious there are three big ones right in the center of your forehead. Something inside you will feel restless and dissatisfied when you get a useless critique, even if it's positive.

It's important to trust your intuition. If you're not being defensive, you'll be able to recognize helpful criticism. You'll light up when you're given insights that show you how to take your story from good to excellent.

And in the end, the most important critique you'll ever get will come from yourself. After all, you're the one who knows the most about the story you're writing. You're the one who knows how you want readers to feel.

Critique groups. Writing groups are designed to provide regular critique for the members.

In an ideal group, laughter overflows as insights roll. Incisive comments are handed out with respect, gratefully received, and weighed within each writer's sense of purpose. Individual strengths are honored, and a context of trust and enjoyment propels the members forward. Supportive synergy surges through the group, leading individuals to create more and write better. Writers who are part of a functional group can grow exponentially, and fast. Well-founded critique is the absolute best way to improve.

But not every group will work out. Sometimes members will give you destructive or useless criticism. Sometimes personalities clash. After all, there isn't a "writer" personality. You don't automatically share traits, values or visions with someone just because you're both interested in writing.

Or you could get wildly inconsistent feedback. Member A thinks your wording is purple, Member B says it's too stark, Member C has no idea what you're trying to say, Member D is sure you've spelled everything out too plainly... You're left dazed and confused. Getting mired in conflicting opinions won't help you. It could even lead to losing sight of your story.

Finding the group that's right for you is a little like dating. Start with pieces of writing that don't matter much while you get a feeling for who you're dealing with. It's hard to know in advance who will be capable of giving perceptive criticism. Even if every member of a group is well-read, a well-read person is not necessarily a good writer any more than a movie buff is a good actor. To further complicate matters, not every good writer has a flair for critique.

Critique groups, like families, have different sets of rules. Some groups operate well within a highly defined structure. For example, a particular format is followed every time. The person receiving a critique may not be allowed to speak. The critique itself must be worded with something positive first, something less positive second, and something more positive to finish up. This is a good idea, especially for new writers who aren't used to criticism.

Other groups are loose and free-flowing and yet get a lot accomplished. More experienced writers don't necessarily need to have criticism buffered with nice comments. Members who've been together a long time may leap straight to the heart of the critique, allowing the writer to enter the discussion.

Some groups are genre-specific, seeking members with similar writing goals. This makes it harder to find enough members. More important than individual focus is group synergy, compatibility, and trust.

Trust is a big factor in effective group dynamics, and different people have different criteria for bestowing trust. For me the big three requirements are honest criticism, respect, and confidentiality. I want to know my fellow writers will lay it on the line and won't be offended when I do the same. I want to be sure we'll all refrain from blabbing outside the group about what is discussed inside. It goes without saying that each writer makes the call on what to keep and what to throw away, including criticism.

If you want to be part of a critique group but you can't find one in your area, consider forming your own. Professional organizations such as Society of Children's Book Writers and Illustrators can put you in touch with writers looking for community.

There are dozens upon dozens of ways to organize critique groups. As I see it, so long as members find help to write better and keep going, the format is secondary. If you operate well in groups, keep looking until you find a place where you fit.

Writing buddies. Working with one or two writing buddies is my personal preference. It's a fantastic way to keep momentum going. For one thing, if I know my buddies are preparing new chapters and going to the trouble of getting to our rendezvous, I'm not going to let them down by procrastinating, getting distracted or backpedaling. I look forward to reading their work, hearing about their week, listening to their insightful wisecracks. We keep each other accountable to the goals we've set.

It's a lifestyle.

How do you find those special individuals who may become as important to you as your marriage partner? Is it too hokey to say "When the writer is ready, the buddy appears?"

If you're dedicated to your craft and wish for companionship within the writing lifestyle, I think you're bound to find kindred fools who love words as much as you do. At least that's how it has worked for me.

Should you hire a book doctor? A number of writers and editors make themselves available to "doctor" your manuscript. This can involve anything from improving and reorganizing the structure of your manuscript to rewriting your book.

Writers are notoriously insecure. Industries have grown up around this fact. When it comes to book doctoring, buyer beware. Questionable and inflated fees arise in this domain sometimes.

Maybe I'm out of line here, but if you really need a book doctor, why not hire a ghostwriter and quit calling yourself a writer? Either you have the gumption and artistry to learn the writing craft or you don't. If you want to learn and you have some aptitude, you'll get there. It will take perseverance, sure. But you will get there. We all reach stagnant, swampy areas when writing. That's no reason to turn your precious story over to someone else.

That said, if you still want to bring a book doctor on board your project, please be careful. Don't pay jaw-dropping fees of thousands of dollars. Is the person qualified? Does he or she claim to have been an editor at a publishing house? Ask for proof. Does the person claim to be an author? Look at his or her work. Anyone can apply for an ISBN, self-publish and claim to be an author. Some self-published books are outstanding, but others are garbage and shouldn't qualify someone to rewrite your book. Dig a little before you shell out your hard-earned cash.

But what if you sense a flaw in your style and can't quite put your finger on it—and you want someone qualified to give an opinion? In that case, a professional critique might be worth getting. There are authors with a real gift for editing who offer paid critiques of the first twenty pages or so of a novel, and for a reasonable fee (no more than a hundred dollars). If you're lucky, you'll gain perspective on getting your novel into shape.

Honing your craft is a must. Your story deserves your best writing, and there are loads of resources around to help you improve. All approaches are valid so long as they get you to write your book. However you learn best, whatever gets you to practice most, do it.

And keep going.

CHAPTER FIVE

SUBMITTING *your* MANUSCRIPT

Submitting *your* Manuscript

No tears in the writer, no tears in the reader.
No surprise for the writer, no surprise for the reader.
— Robert Frost

Writing is to publishing as cooking in your own kitchen is to running a busy downtown restaurant, as singing in the shower is to performing in a stadium, as a small beloved pet is to a great big zoo.

Not the same.

Some writers are content to write purely for the sake of getting the story down. Publishing doesn't interest them. My grandmother was that way. She wrote wonderful stories for her children and grandchildren without a thought of offering them for publication. If you're like her, you'll miss all the entanglements of the business side of things. That's perfectly okay. You might be happier, too.

But most of us want to be published and get our books out there. This chapter outlines the gritty process of submitting your manuscript. If you're a veteran writer familiar with queries, synopses, and agents, this will all be review for you. But if you're new to the submission process, you may benefit from the guided tour.

Agents

Publishing editors are deluged with submissions. Consequently, most large publishing houses have chosen to cut off access to writers who are not already represented by an agent. Thus, if you want an editor at a large publishing house to consider your book for publication, the next step after finishing your manuscript is finding a literary agent.

The difference between literary agents and editors is that literary agents represent authors, and editors represent publishing houses. Editors *acquire* manuscripts. Agents *represent* manuscripts. Literary agents sell manuscripts to publishers on your behalf. They know how to negotiate for you, because they're experienced with elements of the market you may not understand, elements such as royalty advances, foreign rights, audio and screen rights, contracts, etc.

Your agent is invested in you. Agents are paid a fixed percentage of an author's earnings (between 10% and 20%). An ideal agent believes in your work, is well connected in the industry, has a good idea of where your book would find a market, understands contracts and clauses, and manages time effectively. Such a person is invaluable to your career.

So how do you approach an agent you hope will represent you? If the process is new to you, here's a list you may find helpful.

Write the best book you can write. This might sound like a "duh" piece of advice, but it's number one for a reason. You'll be up against hundreds, if not thousands, of other submissions in the course of a single month. You've got to write something that stands out.

Agents lament the volume of submissions they receive that are riddled with grammatical errors and typos, not to mention poor plotting, weak characterization, dull dialogue, lackluster setting, ambiguous point of view, jumbled style, incoherent voice.

If your book has an obvious problem in the first chapter, an agent won't read far enough to find out your second chapter is fabulous. The majority of manuscripts are rejected based on the first page. True! The first agent who agreed to read my first book sent me a rejection slip the same day she received the manuscript. At the time, I was naïve enough to wonder how she could have read the whole thing so fast.

Agents' days are jam-packed with responsibilities and obligations that have nothing to do with sitting leisurely in a chair reading manuscripts. You've got to hook them with the first page.

Research submission guidelines. Literary agencies have websites listing exactly how they want to be approached, but many writers fail to study submission guidelines and therefore take themselves out of the running.

The first thing to look for is whether the agency deals with YA titles. If so, great. Carefully read submission guidelines and then follow them—to the letter! If an agent requests a single page synopsis, don't fudge it and send five pages. If two sample chapters are allowed, send the first two chapters of your novel. If e-mail queries are not welcome, print out your query letter and send it by snail mail.

Although it's fairly standard for agencies to require a query letter with a synopsis and two sample chapters, don't assume all agencies will be the same. Some ask for a query letter only on first contact. Some ask for a query letter plus a synopsis. Whatever they ask for is what you should send.

I recommend *Guide to Literary Agents* (F & W Publications), a book that lists agencies, the genres they represent, style preferences, and submission guidelines or how to obtain them.

Other ways to find good agents include looking on the acknowledgments page of books by writers you admire, to see if they have mentioned their agent. (Please do not e-mail writers and ask for contact information for their agents. This is inappropriate, and will not win you friends.) You can also search the Internet, go to writers' conferences, and hear about good agents via word of mouth.

Study how to write query letters. Every submission you make, whether by e-mail or hard copy, requires a query letter. A query is your formal introduction to yourself and your work. Queries are deceptively difficult to write because you have to figure out how to say, "I've written a book. Would you like to read it?" in a fresh, enticing style. You have to blow your horn without sounding like you're blowing your horn. You must be pithy without being curt. Yeesh!

When writing a query, the basic outline is this: establish a connection with the agent—either by reminding him or her of when and how you met, or by giving a simple, brief explanation of why you've chosen that particular agency. Then, in one paragraph, make your pitch about your book.

Next, list your writing credits—publications, awards and honors, and contests won—unless they're obscure or outdated. (Don't launch into an impassioned autobiography about how much writing means to you. This is unprofessional.)

Close with appreciation. Attach your synopsis and/or sample chapters, if requested. After your signature, clearly show your contact information.

For more information on query letters, read *How To Write Attention Grabbing Queries and Cover Letters*, by John Wood. It is not tailored to YA, but it is very good.

Here's the body of a query letter from aspiring young adult novelist, Rebecca J. Rowley:

It was wonderful to meet you at the Rocky Mountain Fiction Writers annual conference in September. I had the chance to make a pitch to you about my young adult novel titled *My Way Home*, and you kindly invited me to follow up with you.

My Way Home explores the lengths to which a pregnant teen will go to find acceptance after her family rejects her. Fifteen and pregnant, Reagan Stiles longs to find support and acceptance from her estranged older sister before her water breaks. Leaving her grandmother's care, Reagan seeks out her sister, Kyla. Instead of offering open arms, Kyla panics and sends her away. Upon returning home, Reagan learns the boy who impregnated her has fathered a second child. Devastated by their son's irresponsibility, his family takes Reagan in. His parents try to make her feel welcome, but this temporary home does not satisfy her desire for belonging. She continues pursuing her sister and uncovers the secret that created their divide. Once the truth is known, Reagan has a choice of whether to forgive her sister and renew their bond, or forge an alliance with the family providing obligatory support.

A portion of this novel was awarded Honorable Mention in the 75th Annual Writer's Digest Writing Competition in November 2006 and Honorable Mention in the ACC Writers Studio 2007 Literary Contest announced in March 2007.

A synopsis and two sample chapters accompany this letter. I appreciate your time in considering my work.

If you receive a positive response to a query, you're ready for the next hurdle—you get to send your entire book, either as an attached file or as hard copy, depending on what the agent prefers. After that, expect to wait another two to six months before you hear back from the agent. Don't call about it unless six months have gone by. Then you can make one phone call or send one polite e-mail asking about the status.

Be ready to make a verbal pitch. What is a verbal pitch? It's not singing. It's not baseball. It's not singing about baseball...Those of you who have attended writers' conferences know exactly what I'm talking about. A verbal pitch amounts to an in-person query. In a brief speech, you tell an agent or editor about your book.

Verbal pitches often take place by appointment at writers' conferences. (Occasionally they happen more spontaneously—during mixers or dinner conversations.) A scheduled pitch will typically allow writers between five and fifteen minutes with an editor or agent. One to five minutes are allocated to make the pitch itself, with the rest of the time assigned for feedback and conversation.

Easy as pie.

Ha!

I've seen writers get sick over verbal pitches. Sweaty palms, trembling voice, and overwhelming nausea. No wonder. How do you sum up your whole book in a couple of sentences without sounding rehearsed and wooden?

A tall order, for sure. It's natural to be nervous. But verbal pitches are definitely worth doing. If you impress an agent or editor with your personality and story ideas, you've transformed yourself from a complete unknown to a person of positive interest.

My best advice here is to prepare a good log line (defined below), and then relax. Be friendly and professional. The agent or editor is there because he or she is looking for great manuscripts—and you're there because you have a wonderful story to offer. A perfect match.

In case you haven't come across the term "log line"—a log line (aka tag line) is a sentence or two that sums up your story in an enticing way. For example, in Rebecca J. Rowley's query letter on page 92, the log line for her novel *My Way Home* is, "Fifteen and pregnant, Reagan Stiles longs to find support and acceptance from her estranged older sister before her water breaks." My log line for *The Seer and the Sword* is, "A prince born to peace and privilege loses his father, his kingdom, his sword, and his freedom. How does he rise to become the most famous warrior of his time?"

Most novelists are not by nature concise. We love words—at length. So writing a pithy log line can be challenging. But take the challenge. You'll be glad you did. Then, when someone asks what your book is about, instead of staring blankly ahead with nothing but "uh" on your tongue, or launching into a rambling chapter-by-chapter description, you can bring out your beautifully evocative log line.

During your verbal pitch, you may be asked about something known as your "platform." Not shoes with mighty big heels. Not your political stance. The agent or editor you're speaking with wants to know how/if your background and previous writing experience will give you credibility and help market your book.

For example, when I pitched *Wild Ink* I mentioned that I've led well-attended workshops at writers' conferences on how to write for teenagers. I've worked with thousands of teens in writing workshops for school and library programs over seven years. Reading other writers of young adult literature is a hobby and a great pleasure for me, and many of those writers might (and did!) contribute interviews for my proposed book. Also, I've hosted a radio program about writing, called *The Page Turner*. Finally, all three of my fiction books have been finalists for the

Colorado Blue Spruce award, a list chosen solely by teens themselves. That was my platform for *Wild Ink*.

Laura Resau's books, including *What the Moon Saw* and *Red Glass*, feature modern American teens visiting South America. Resau is a bilingual anthropologist. She spent two years in the mountainous Mixtec region of Oaxaca, Mexico. Her education and travels lend credibility to her stories—an example of a platform for fiction.

Admittedly, it's easier to build a logical platform for nonfiction than fiction—and when *The Seer and the Sword* was first written, I had no platform to speak of. I'd never entered a fiction contest, never attended a writers' conference. Didn't know diddly. So if you're in a similar boat, don't worry. A book can still float simply because it does.

Practice your pitch. Get comfortable with the idea of "talking up" your manuscript. And there's a lovely book about the subject, called *Making the Perfect Pitch: How to Catch a Literary Agent's Eye*, by Katharine Sands.

Learn how to write a synopsis. With any manuscript you complete, you are going to need a synopsis.

A synopsis is a summary of your book, telling all the main points about what happens, from beginning to end. Written in present tense, the synopsis cannot include any dialogue.

Why do you need a synopsis? Because literary agents and editors will ask for one. They like to look at a synopsis to see if your story hangs together.

Many writers, myself included, find it harder to write a synopsis than an entire novel. It isn't easy to condense all the nuance and craft you've put into your book into a brief story in present tense. It's tricky to get the feeling of the book into a few pages—and conveying the feeling is a big part of your job.

I highly recommend Pam McCutcheon's book, *Writing the Fiction Synopsis*. McCutcheon clearly presents all the information you'll need to write your own synopsis. It is well worth the price.

Remember that agents are not obligated to respond. When you approach an agent who hasn't asked you to submit a query, you're in a category known as unsolicited submissions. Some agencies do not accept unsolicited material at all. Doing your homework will help you make good use of your valuable time.

Agents are overwhelmed with submissions. Depending on the agency, expect to wait 4-12 months for an answer to your query. Don't try to make your manuscript stand out with gimmicks like colored paper, or enclosing confetti or balloons. Don't call the office of someone considering your work. Don't send e-mail after e-mail, cookies, or candy. If they're interested, they'll call you or e-mail you.

Consider submitting to more than one agent at a time. When I began submitting over ten years ago, the standard in the industry was to submit queries to one agent at a time, but the waiting period for rejection/acceptance back then was shorter than it is now.

If published authors are rejected an average of ten times before being accepted and it takes up to a year to get a reply, the math is pretty obvious. Ten years is too long to wait. And once an agent represents you, you'll wait again as your agent submits to publishers on your behalf. This can take from a few weeks to a year. Once a publisher says yes, you'll wait for a contract—between two to twelve months. The contract will specify that your book will be published anywhere from eighteen months to three years from the date of the contract.

Whew! An ironic twist to an industry in which time is of the essence.

Simultaneous submissions may be the way to go, but at the same time, be smart. Research individual agents and craft your queries to reflect their individuality. Don't write a form letter query and then blanket every agent you can find. A generic letter is easy to spot. It will tell agents you haven't done your homework. This is important.

If, after sending out several carefully researched query packages, you end up with more than one agent who wants to represent you, you have a hot story. How do you decide which agent to choose? That's a problem you want to have!

Understand that an agent will assess the commercial value of your manuscript. If only marketing were not the last word in publishing, how different the world would be. Lack of marketability automatically excludes some wonderful books.

But publishing is a business and the object of the game for the publisher is to make money.

The publishing industry is in the midst of change as it continues to adjust to the implications of the Internet and other e-technology. Once upon a time, books, newspapers, and magazines were the province of the printed word. Now the Internet is a vast storehouse of information, offering fierce—and free—competition for the publishing industry. It's an e-explosion.

Publishers are not designed to be lending institutions for artistic endeavors, and the days when large houses published books solely upon literary merit without a marketing angle are fading fast. Publishers are now forced, by the nature of the game they're in, to gamble heavily on books, losing money on roughly seven out of ten, breaking even on about two out of ten, and making money on only ten percent.

To a publisher your art is a product first and foremost. It has to be.

Another way to look at it: If you belong to a writing group or class where you've had the opportunity to read unpublished writing, or if you've read fan fiction online, you know that some of it is well done. But would you pay for it? If the answer is yes, take it one step further and ask yourself if you'd invest money to print and market the work in hopes of getting a return. That's the question publishing houses must answer every day. Agents who decide to represent you must be convinced they can sell your work. They must be able to confidently ask a publishing house to gamble—on you!

Another factor in commercial viability (or lack thereof): an agent may have recently signed an author who offered a project similar to yours. This is where luck enters the picture. Let's say you've submitted a brilliant book about triplets who explore string theory together once they've discovered their unusual genes give them the ability to slip in and out of other dimensions. But the agent has just worked hard to sell another series about twins who double for each other while slipping in and out of alternate realities. Though not exactly the same, the books are too similar to find a market with the same agent.

This really does happen. All the time. It's the luck of the draw, baby! But if you get a short note saying an agent liked your writing style but has a similar project in the works, take heart. Whoever took time out of a busy schedule to write you an individualized note meant every word. You write well enough to be worthy of encouragement from a professional.

Another dragon in the publishing world is trends. As discussed in Chapter Three, you may have written an excellent historical novel during a time in publishing when historical novels for teens are considered passé. Your book might have taken the world by storm ten years ago or ten years hence, but right now it's not likely to get a hearing.

What happens if you receive a rejection letter with a note saying the person considering your work loved it but doesn't believe it has enough market appeal?

You could wrack your brain for a marketing angle and then try to persuade whoever has rejected you of the merits of your plan. The chances of succeeding with that approach hover between zero and minus one, so it's probably a waste of time.

You could humbly ask if there's anything you can do to ratchet up the market value of your work—in a letter, of course, not a phone call. Then listen to suggestions. Maybe revisions are in order. Perhaps if you subtract a few peaceful scenes in favor of more action—or change the ending—you might begin to see how your story could be stronger and better. Tackle revisions gratefully.

Then again, maybe an agent asks you to rethink your entire premise, remove your true voice, or turn your female protagonist into a male. . .

Now we're getting into a tricky area. You want to be an author and get published, but at what price? At what point do reasonable requests to improve your story turn into demands to sell out in ways you can't live with?

Personally, I listen very closely to everything I'm told, and then let my soul be my pilot.

Realize that agents are people, and tastes differ. What sings to one agent drones to another. Naturally, you're looking for someone simpatico with your story and style. Sometimes this process takes a while! Just keep your head, your heart— and your patience, if you can.

Is an agent essential?

Sometimes authors meet an editor of a publishing company, form a direct connection, and sign a contract without agent representation. If a publisher allows you to represent yourself, you'll want to be able to read and understand contracts, and have reason to trust the publisher who wants your book. An agent is not required— but an agent makes the whole process easier for many reasons. Agents know the market. They know what is realistic. They're highly trained professionals, and they're in your corner.

To submit to an editor rather than an agent, all the advice on submitting to agents applies.

Agents—in Their Own Words

To get a sense of what really goes on in an agent's life, I interviewed three agents who represent young adult novels. Their words follow.

Edina Imrik

Ed Victor Literary Agency

Edina Imrik does not accept unsolicited queries.

What makes a manuscript stand out for you? What characteristics—other than good writing—make you sit up and take notice?

Having a strong narrative voice is important from page one. However, writing is such a subjective business, every person will favor different things. Even if the work is well-written it may not be picked up by the first agent who reads it so it is worth sending it to a few people.

What are some of the most common mistakes writers make when writing YA? When sending in manuscripts?

One of the most common mistakes writers can make is not researching their intended readership enough. How could anyone write for a specific age group if they don't know what they like to read? Books, just like everything in the world, are changing all the time and it is important to keep up with what is out there. Research is also important when submitting a manuscript to an agent. The writer needs to find out the name of the person they want to send their work to and if they are willing to consider unsolicited manuscripts. If the answer is yes, they need to find out what material the agent needs—usually three sample chapters and a synopsis. It is important also to send a stamped envelope big enough for the return of the work, or state in your letter that you do not want your work returned—this is common courtesy. Another mistake is sending

random chapters, rather than the first three. Nobody should do this—random chapters don't make sense. If the first three chapters are not good enough to be sample chapters, they need to be rewritten.

Is there something about the life of an agent that you wish more writers knew about or understood?

There is ample resource material about the role of the literary agent, so I am not going into that. Most of us are very busy and work hard on defending and promoting the interests of our existing clients, and any new reading we do is in our spare time. Each of us personally receives about 5-10 submissions a day. It is simply impossible to read every single page—therefore, the first few pages are crucial in our decision to read on or not.

How much weight do you give to a synopsis as opposed to sample chapters?

This is entirely up to personal preference. I personally read the chapters first and if it intrigues me, I like to see how the rest of the book will work before asking for the whole script. I normally never ask for more than a one-page synopsis.

If you could suggest one thing that would help writers find success, what would it be?

Write an interesting and engaging cover letter with your submission—it is the first thing the agent will see and the more you engage them, the more likely they will read on.

Q&A

Anita Kushen

Anita Kushen & Associates
www.anitakushen.com

Anita Kushen vetted manuscripts for new authors in her spare time for almost twenty years while she owned and ran three businesses, taught ESL for the US Army and the state of Texas, worked as a makeup person for summer stock and manned rape crisis and suicide hotlines. She slowed down long enough to have two sons and raised them while teaching at Mile High Academy in Denver and Arapahoe Community College in Littleton, Colorado. One day she awoke to two grown boys with lives of their own and asked herself, "Now what?" and Anita Kushen & Associates, Inc. (AKA) was born.

What makes a manuscript stand out for you? What characteristics—other than good writing—make you sit up and take notice?

Well-developed characters, interaction, flow, attention grabbing page turner, sustaining interest through suspense, conflict, humor.

What are some of the most common mistakes writers make when writing for teens?

Speaking in an immature tone, oversimplification, overuse of slang and trend.

Is there something about the life of an agent that you wish more writers knew about or understood?

The life of an agent is extremely busy, and authors need to have patience and let us do our jobs.

How much weight do you give to a synopsis as opposed to sample chapters?

The synopsis is important to understand the entirety of the story and know what the different aspects and events are that occur in the novel. The sample chapters weigh heavier as they show the writer's ability to carry a reader through a story and write in an intriguing and professional manner.

If you could suggest one thing that would help writers find success, what would it be?

Join a writers' critique group, and read a lot of books in the genre you are writing in. The more opinions you can collect and the more feedback you receive, the more likely it is your book will be clear and well-rounded enough to appeal to the large audience you will need to capture. Also, make sure your work is edited and clean. Small mistakes and grammatical errors can distract a reader enough to take away from your story. Be passionate about what you are writing; you need to be invested in your story. If you write about something important and moving, your passion will pass on to the reader and create the magical connection that is vital to success for a novel.

Q & A

AGENT Q&A

Lilly Ghahremani

Full Circle Literary Agency
www.fullcircleliterary.com

After graduating UCLA School of Law, Lilly Ghahremani soon decided to "use her powers for good," representing authors across a variety of genres. She is always interested in well-paced young adult fiction, multicultural themes and characters, and explorations of the undiscovered facets of teen life. (She says that a witty and self-deprecating character will always catch her attention!) Her agency is always happy to add talented new YA authors.

What makes a manuscript stand out for you? What characteristics—other than good writing—make you sit up and take notice?

We all say the same thing—that a manuscript stands out for us when it keeps us up at night. But what does that mean? In the YA genre, the most important thing you can do is create a character we can relate to. Does your character have interesting quirks and flaws? Is she a compelling, interesting, observant person? For my own taste, I'm a huge fan of humor—there is so much in adolescence to poke fun at, and I love when authors indulge themselves. What will make me take notice is strong writing combined with a youthful voice. Sometimes we'll receive a beautifully polished manuscript, but it's clear that the (adult) author is the ventriloquist. Keep an eye out for little slips—did you accidentally use a phrase from the 80s that our fearless protagonist would never have known (because she wasn't alive yet!), etc? Those sorts of slips take me right out of the moment.

For me, the beauty of the teenage years is the incredibly weird and unique worlds we create for ourselves at that age. I love to be invited into a world that wasn't my own but to be invited in a way that makes me want to stick around.

What are some of the most common mistakes writers make when writing YA? When sending in manuscripts?

As I mentioned above, writers with the best of intentions will accidentally give an adult voice to the teen genre. Don't get me wrong—our teen readers are brilliant and mature, but there are certain ways they wouldn't speak—such as the way their 55-year-old author would, etc. It's common to see adult writers slip out of voice or write in a voice they think teen readers will relate to. The worst thing a writer can do is lose touch with their audience, to write in a cave. The best YA writers are those who are reading current YA, and paying attention to how the YA market is growing and changing. What magazines does your target reader read? Are you reading them? Are you watching their shows? Do you really "get" them or are you trying too hard to be the "cool" adult and not putting in the time?!

Another mistake I see is trying to be provocative for provocation's sake. People constantly ask me if they should write edgy since "edgy sells." But with the process of publication taking as long as it can, your book may not hit shelves for a while. Write something that is timeless. If you're going to be edgy, do it because your story requires it, and because you feel deep down that that is the most sincere way to tell your tale.

I'm also iffy on dating a book. Too many Lindsay Lohan/Aaron Carter references can date a book unnecessarily.

Regarding mistakes upon submission, I'd say:

- Being overly eager (aka The "Red Flag" mistake). You want agents to take their time and read your submission. If you "nudge" them before the 4-6 week mark and if you consistently badger them with e-mails, you will ensure your quick relegation to the pass pile.

- Not checking what the agent accepts (aka the "Waste of Time" mistake). Make sure you're sending your wonderful YA manuscript to

the appropriate agent. Make sure you're pursuing agents who are as excited about the YA market as you are.

- Not being familiar with the genre (aka the "Amateur" mistake). If you are undertaking YA authorship as a serious career, you need to devote the time and energy to getting to know your industry as much as any other profession. What books are exciting young readers? Read about them in *Publishers Weekly*, and be sure to rub elbows with local librarians and bookstore salespeople. They know what is happening on the ground, and you should, too.

Is there something about the life of an agent that you wish more writers knew about or understood?

I wish authors knew how difficult our job can be. Our job is to pick out, not only what's "good" but what is so excellent that we would stake our reputation (and time) on it. We work on commission, so we have to pick up projects we feel we can be fully invested in for however long it takes to find them that right home. On the flip side, you, the author, deserve an agent who feels that same excitement you do about the potential for your work. Ultimately I wish authors knew that an agent's response isn't a reflection on their eventual success. It's a reflection of our workload and our own enthusiasm.

I often explain to my classes that our evaluation of a manuscript is exactly what you do at the bookstore—you pick it up, you read through a few pages, and if you're not really feeling invested in taking it to the counter, you don't. You want to match up with the reader who can't wait to pay and hunker down with your novel, not the person who felt pressured to buy because it was at a sale price!!! It's worth waiting for the perfect agent. We all work very very hard, but you need more than just a hard worker. You need that perfect person.

Writers should also know that this is a small industry, so take deep breaths before sending "revenge" e-mails.

We're all in this industry because books mean the world to us. Agents work around the clock to be sure there are new books for our readers. You may reconnect with an agent on another project (this has certainly happened for me) or you may run into him or her along the line. Stay positive and move forward. The perfect agent is out there.

How much weight do you give to a synopsis as opposed to sample chapters?

I absolutely give sample chapters more weight. Sure, I have to be interested in the storyline, but I get a sense of that from the query already. The pages are what really count to me. Do I keep reading the submission because I can't stop myself, or am I reading because I was promised something good in the synopsis? I don't want to get stuck in that situation, so I read the book for the book and usually keep the synopsis to the side, just in case I need a refresher.

And as far as format, I honestly don't mind what format a synopsis comes in (although 20 page chapter-by-chapter synopses are a bit much, and I imagine a nightmare to draft).

If you could suggest one thing that would help writers find success, what would it be?

I think a good attitude will get you very far in this industry. It sounds cheesy, I know. But it encompasses many elements—staying open to criticism and feedback, realizing there are possibilities and that "where a window closes, a door opens" (ie., if an agent passes on your book, it might just mean a better agent for you is yet to come!), and to stay confident. We need wonderful books for our young readers. You are doing an important—no, crucial—thing in writing them. Good deeds are rewarded.

* * * * *

Things to Watch Out For

The publishing game is complex. When you're new to the game, it's possible to make some big mistakes. Here are a couple of scams to be alert for.

"Agent" scams. Because so many writers are trying to break into print, the publishing industry has attracted its share of unscrupulous people trying to take advantage of naiveté. Some do this by calling themselves agents when they're nothing of the sort. If an "agent" does any of the following, get out without looking back:

- The "agent" collects reading fees. In other words, you are charged money because the agent has read your book. Legitimate literary agencies do not charge for reading your work. The Association of Authors' Representatives Canon of Ethics specifically prohibits agents from collecting reading fees from clients or potential clients.

- The "agent" offers you a contract that penalizes you or charges you should the agent fail to sell your work in a specified period. This is not a professional practice among agents. Always read contracts with care.

- The "agent" gets cagey about revealing other clients and makes excuses when asked for references. Established agents are proud of their clients.

- The "agent" asks for money up front to offset the costs of marketing your manuscript. Reputable agents do not charge up front. They make their money from a percentage of your sales. If they must buy extra copies of your book to market to foreign countries or have other extra expenses, they might charge you costs but they will subtract those amounts from advances or royalties.

A true agent will help you more than you can imagine. Unfortunately, anyone can list him/herself as an agent, so be careful out there.

Writing contests. Another scam to watch for is bogus writing contests. Whereas winning large scale and well-regarded writing contests can give you something to put in your query letter to catch an agent's eye, please don't get scammed into sending exorbitant entry fees to Jack The Writer's website contest. (As of this writing, a reasonable amount for an entry fee is between ten and twenty-five bucks, depending on the reputation of the contest.) And don't ever sign away your rights to a contest.

Winning a contest given by an obscure or unknown group won't help your chances of finding representation with an agent. To be worth your while, a writing contest should be run by a large magazine, a publishing company, a college or university, or an established writers' conference. Entries should be judged by qualified people. This is more rare than you might think. Authors are busy, and many of us have no time to judge contests.

I've never entered a fiction writing contest. But I've read remarks from several contest judges about other entries submitted by friends. Some of these judges—unpublished themselves—have given what I consider to be appallingly bad advice. Some seemed interested in crushing the aspirations of the entrant into dust.

However, if you want to add credibility to a blank writing resumé, winning a big contest can help. For example, *Writer's Digest* sponsors several annual writing contests that are nationally known. And if you were to rack up several wins at conferences such as Pike's Peak Writers Conference or San Francisco Writers Conference—which have good national reputations—all the better.

But keep in mind it isn't necessary to win contests to get published. And getting slammed by a judge who isn't published either is not conducive to your goals. Or peace of mind.

Writing Journeys

I thought it might be interesting to hear the inside scoop from writers who are at the stage of the process where they've caught the attention of an agent but don't yet have a book contract. On the following pages are four interviews with aspiring young adult novelists.

Q&A

AUTHOR Q&A

Coleen DeGroff

Has an agent

Has won major writing contests

No book contract—yet

How did you go about finding an agent?

It took me many many years, tons of postage and a stack of rejections massive enough to insulate my entire home before I landed an agent. I could have saved myself all kinds of money and avoided numerous restraining orders if I'd waited until my writing was of publishable quality before I began submitting to agents and editors. Then again, if I wasn't delusional enough to think I could do this, I never would have attempted it in the first place.

I met my agent at the Big Sur Children's Writing Workshop several years ago. She signed me on as her client based on a YA manuscript I'd written called *Skipping Stones*, which chronicled the tale of a teen girl who lost her mother and journeyed to find her way back from grief to a new life. Although the manuscript received much positive feedback from editors and even went through an acquisitions meeting at a major publisher, it ultimately didn't sell. My agent pulled me off the ledge and told me not to freak out, that it's often the second or third or, God forbid, even the *fourth* manuscript which ends up selling first.

Neurotic mess that I am, of course I didn't believe her but I started working on a new manuscript anyway. Which is how *Liberty Belz and the Suburb of Doom*, the story of a circus family who runs away to the suburbs, came about. Apparently there aren't a lot of smartass books out there featuring a 13-year-old protagonist who holds the dubious honor of being the first person born into a world famous trapeze family who's afraid of heights, because the next thing

I knew, it won the San Francisco Writers Contest and the Pikes Peak Writers Contest in the YA category.

Where do things stand now with your book?

My agent loves it, several editors have expressed an interest, and now I'm just waiting for the big money to roll on in!!

What has helped you the most in learning to write for young adults?

Not being popular. Not having breasts. Not being invited to the prom. Not being mentioned in people's yearbook write-ups. Not being able to throw overhand. Not being part of "the" group...all of those things, coupled with a serious case of arrested development and a reservoir of snappy comebacks that I always wanted to use but never had the nerve to say...these are the things that drive my writing.

What setbacks have you faced?

Besides crippling self-doubt, family crises, and occasional struggles with clinical depression? None come to mind.

For you, what's the easiest part of writing?

I wouldn't say any of it is easy, but certainly I have the most fun writing when the characters come alive inside my mind and start running around and I just get to sit back and take notes.

What's the hardest thing about writing?

When the characters sit down and glare at me and say "You're the writer. You tell us what comes next!" That's the point where coffee and chutzpah (hopefully) carry me through to the other side of the dead zone. Sometimes the process takes longer than others, but in the end it all works out.

Q&A

Olgy Maria Aleu (aka Olgy Gary)

Has an agent
Has placed in a major writing contest
No book contract—yet

How did you go about finding an agent?

Several agents as well as editors have asked to see my manuscript once it's completed. I've found them all by attending writing conferences. In particular, during the 2002 conference of the Rocky Mountain Chapter of the Society of Children's Book Writers and Illustrators (SCBWI). I found myself sitting with an agent who began asking question after question about what it was like to live in Cuba when Fidel Castro took power in 1959. As I responded I realized I was describing chapters in the book I wanted to write. It was validating to receive confirmation, from someone familiar with publishing giants, that mine was a story worth telling. I remember going to sleep that night wondering if I'd made it all up. Was the agent really excited to read *Island of My Heart*?

The next morning he gave me his business card, saying he wanted my story. He gave me his e-mail, several phone numbers and told me to call him if I got stuck while writing it.

With three-fourths of *Island of My Heart* completed, I entered it in the 2005 Paul Gillette Writing Contest, sponsored by the Pikes Peak Writers Conference. It won second place in the YA division, and a second agent asked to see it. I've pitched the story idea to several editors as well. They've asked to see the manuscript when completed.

Where do things stand now with your book?

I've promised myself 2008 is the year I'll finish writing the book. *Island of My Heart* is not only the working title of my novel, but also

AUTHOR Q&A

115

the sentiment millions of Cubans in the exiled community have about their homeland. My book is the story of a 12-year-old girl in Cuba when Castro takes over. All the events I share in the novel I've matched with historical dates/events in the history of Cuba from 1959 through 1963. The girl in this novel loves to read fantasy and fairy tales. From that world, she draws the strength to make it in the real life/death struggle that overtakes her island paradise. The manuscript is now 80% completed.

What has helped you the most in learning to write for young adults?

Reading voraciously for as long as I can remember. I love science fiction and fantasy, always have, always will. Growing up in Cuba, sci-fi/fantasy was my window to the world of "what if." Regardless of what was happening around me in the turbulent years after Castro came to power, my voracious reading brought a measure of peace to my 12-year-old heart.

Wanting to write and learning to write aren't synonymous. My love of reading made me want to write, but my involvement in the writing community gave me the focus and knowledge to get started and carry on. Being a full SCBWI member as well as sponsoring writers groups through my organization ChildrenComeFirst.com have all helped me fine-tune my writing skills.

What setbacks have you faced?

In life? Too many to recount! Ha! But I've been lucky enough to turn my love for writing into paying jobs as author, editor, ghostwriter, and translator.

For you, what's the easiest part of writing?

I love public speaking, and I think of writing as speaking with my fingers rather than my vocal chords. When I write, I envision the audience and write them a love letter, so to speak. In my mind, both speaking and writing need to be uplifting,

mesmerizing, empowering, and life-giving. My writing is meant to do this as much as my speaking engagements.

As I learn more about the craft of writing, the process becomes more enjoyable. Writing is hard work and you either do the work beforehand (plotting) or afterwards (rewriting). I like doing the work beforehand and my first drafts evolve s-l-o-w-l-y but when I'm done with them they're more like a third or fourth draft.

What's the hardest thing about writing?

Writing, in general, is not hard for me. I'm an author, game designer, editor, ghostwriter and educational consultant. I hold an M.A. in Instructional Design, with an emphasis on cross-cultural communication. I maintain several author and educational sites, including my own. I love working with words and creating word pictures. However, it's a different story when it comes to writing this book so very dear and close to my heart. I find it hard somehow to justify setting aside time for my own dream when I have a list of clients paying me to write for them, edit or translate their manuscripts.

I will finish, though. I must.

Q&A

Rebecca J. Rowley

Has placed in major writing contests
No book contract—yet

What is your involvement in the writing community?

Since early childhood I've been a writer, a storyteller, and a bit of a gossip. I was born into it and realized young that this was not a path I had a choice about traveling, but one I had to take to survive—or else the stories stockpiling in my head would cause severe cranial damage. In my mid-teens my passion found focus. Now, a dozen novel drafts, over 100 short stories, and four screenplays later, I proudly bear the chronic calluses of the committed scribe.

I recently received 3rd place for short fiction in the 2008 Unknown Writers' Contest sponsored by the Denver Woman's Press Club. A portion of my current young adult novel in progress was awarded Honorable Mention in the 75th Annual Writer's Digest Writing Competition in November 2006 and Honorable Mention in the ACC Writers Studio 2007 Literary Contest announced in March 2007. My previous publishing credits include poetry and journaling samples in national magazines.

Where do things stand now with your YA book?

The book is under consideration by an agent who will review it again once I've made some suggested tweaks and shuffles.

What has helped you the most in learning to write?

Shoe commercials. In the words of Nike advertisers: "Just do it!"...and trusted mentors on call to help me work through the kinks, tangents, and gasping breaths.

What setbacks have you faced?

No one has taught me how to make a living as a budding writer, so the pursuit of a writing career feels frustrating, because a job means time...time I wish I could use to write. Then there's low self-esteem and doubt to stumble over when my energy's low. One would think I'd add rejection to the list, but I've turned rejection into a game. At fifteen, I told myself I would receive 100 rejections before I got a book published. So now I get excited when I get a "No way" letter. Each one puts me another step closer to the future "Yes, we want you! We have to have you! Can you give us three books by December?"

Bring 'em on! I only need about twenty more.

For you, what's the easiest part of writing?

It justifies my multiple personalities (kidding). What's easy for me is finding my character's voice on the page. Once I'm ready to introduce her to the world, she and I have already traveled through galaxies of dreams. By page one, she's an old friend. I just sit back and listen to her talk.

What's the hardest thing about writing?

Two things. First, following the rules! Your book must have a beginning, middle, AND end. You have to use proper spelling and grammar. You have to show, NOT tell. You can't have all your character names begin with the letter "B." Well, Ben, Bailey, Burt, and Betty don't want to hear it...until revision round 22.

Second, I have trouble keeping up momentum toward the end. The baby's head and shoulders are out, and suddenly I feel as if I just can't push anymore. Being the sort of writer who always has the next project in mind, when I know I'm near completion, the creative devil on my right shoulder starts to lure me away to conceive the next child before the last has left the womb.

Q&A

Amy Koumis

Has an agent
Has won a major writing contest
No book contract—yet

As an eighteen-year-old writer of young adult literature, you're in a rare position because you have an agent. How did you go about finding an agent?

I finished my first novel, a YA fantasy, in 2005 and started shopping it around to agents. My experience with rejection up to that point was mostly limited to contests and things like that, so when the first form letter rejections started showing up, I began to realize that maybe the vision I had of agents climbing over themselves to represent my manuscript might not be realistic.

Another year went by before I accepted that nobody liked book number one. Then I took an idea I had been playing with for a while and wrote a new book. I didn't really expect much, seeing as previous responses were so overwhelmingly negative, so it was a shock when I started receiving "good" rejections, which were basically agents telling me I was good, but not for them. And while I was collecting these, I corresponded with Lilly Ghahremani of Full Circle Literary, whom I had met previously at the Pikes Peak Writers Conference. She was astonishingly nice, and didn't dismiss me right away as a novelty. It was another two months before I signed with her agency, and while this ought to have been a magical solution to all my writerly insecurities, it just made them worse. Now I had something to live up to. It remains to be seen whether or not I actually will.

Where do things stand now with your book?

I was one of those people who thought getting an agent was "the hard part." But my agent pointed out a number of places in my

Q&A

book that could use reworking, and I ended up doing so many revisions that now there's a stack of new drafts going up past my knee. The finished novel—*Spyglass*—went out at last on submission to publishers. No bites yet.

What has helped you the most in learning to write?

I am really, really bad at being scheduled and disciplined when it comes to just about everything, writing included. So one of the things I had to learn early on was how to spend months planning, plotting, writing and rewriting scenes.

Something important I learned to avoid, which seems really common in young writers especially, is mimicking your idols. Tolkien and Rowling are the big ones. When you're bowled over by the awesomeness of someone else's work, it's so easy to want to be just like them that you end up writing just like them. You come off sounding like Tolkien or Rowling, but kind of lukewarm and clammy and not very good. One of the most common things I hear about my writing is, "You have a very clear and original voice." If there is one thing every writer should remember, it's that people pick up your book to read how you write, not how another writer writes.

What setbacks have you faced?

The same ones every writer faces—rejection, envy, despair, insomnia—and, because of my age, a truckload of others on top of that. The big one was school; I found that the more time I spent in a classroom with no control over what I was learning or who I was learning it from took a lot out of me. All I wanted to do was write and draw and tell stories.

Looking back, I realize that even if you do know what you want to do with your life at the age of twelve, it isn't necessarily the best idea to start at the age of twelve. I was going to online school while I was writing my second novel, which I desperately wanted to finish but didn't have the time to work on. So, like a true procrastinator, I skipped school for three weeks and wrote almost solidly, day and night, until I had the completed manu-

script on my computer (for the record, I don't think I changed out of my pajamas for the entire twenty-one days). My grades dropped, and it took me double the amount of time to bring them up again.

I don't regret choosing writing over school, but the road would definitely have been smoother if I'd waited until graduation to start my career.

For you, what's the easiest part of writing?

Getting to live in my imagination. I am a sucker for romance, adventure and fantasy—all the things you can't find in the real world. Getting to put those things on the page however I want, and the feelings that go with it, is the reason I ditched everything else to spend my life chasing that feeling. On the page, I matter, and anything I think becomes what the people in my stories think, how they act and move. It may sound lame to say I don't have any words for when I get in "the zone" and it's just me and the scene playing out in my mind like a movie reel. But it does go beyond words.

What's the hardest thing about writing?

Edits, rejection, more edits, poor sleeping habits, even more edits, deteriorating social skills, deteriorating vision, enduring financial shortages, isolation, boredom, frustration, etc. Everything easy about writing is overshadowed by everything hard about writing. In fact, no one really knows why writers exist at all, aside from it being a known fact that sitting around in your bathrobe all afternoon isn't going to get you a job as a bank manager.

CHAPTER SIX

GETTING *your* BOOK PUBLISHED

GETTING *your* BOOK PUBLISHED

YOU NEED NOT EXPECT TO GET YOUR BOOK RIGHT THE FIRST TIME.
GO TO WORK AND REVAMP OR REWRITE IT.
- MARK TWAIN

WRITE A NOVEL IF YOU MUST, BUT THINK OF MONEY AS AN UNLIKELY ACCIDENT.
GET YOUR REWARD OUT OF WRITING IT, AND TRY TO BE CONTENT WITH THAT.
- PEARL S. BUCK

If you already have a successful writing career in the adult or children's market, you already know the gist of this chapter on publishing. Feel free to skip to the last chapter, which is full of interviews with authors of young adult fiction.

For the many who love to write but don't know much about what happens after getting a "yes" from a publisher, this chapter describes the weird wonders of taking your first flight as an author. We'll explore the view of contracts, editing, cover design, marketing, working with small presses versus large, and interviews with editors in the business.

When I got my first "yes" call, I knew plenty about how to take a flight of fancy but zilch about the publishing plane. I was so ignorant, I was afraid I'd unknowingly commit some heinous gaffe and wind up sailing alone through the empty spaces in my head, oxygen deprived and missing a parachute.

The thing is, people in the publishing industry are far too busy to take each new author by the hand and educate us, yet authors are expected to know what's going on—even when we don't.

I flew by the seat of my pants (something I've had a lot of practice doing)—and learned as I went. You, however, may not want to approach publishing by that method of transport. So if you're curious about what happens after a publisher says "yes," read on.

Contracts and Money

Your book contract will state terms for royalties, advances, and rights. Royalties are the percentage of book sales paid to the author. A variety of amounts can be designated, depending on the publisher, the edition (hardcover or paperback), the publisher's market base, etc. What used to be a standard rate for royalties isn't necessarily standard anymore, because of changes in discounting policies for retailers and other developments in the industry. Therefore, it's impossible to give you a certain figure for what your royalties will be. At the time of this writing, a low end royalty would be 5% of the retail cost of your book. Very high end would be 15%. Whatever the royalty rate, it will be spelled out clearly in your contract. (Note: The structure for royalties and advances from Christian publishers is different from mainstream fiction. The royalty rate is higher but it's based on the wholesale price of the book.)

An advance is the amount the publisher pays you before any sales take place. (Not all publishers pay advances.) Editors arrive at this amount by guessing how many copies of your book can reasonably be expected to sell. Your advance will dovetail with the size of the initial print run planned for your title. A print run is the number of copies of your book your publisher prints at one time.

To determine your advance, the initial print run number is basically multiplied by the projected retail price of your book. That total is then multiplied by your projected royalty rate. Example: A print run of 5000 hardcover copies is planned. The retail price will be about $15.00. The print run multiplied by the retail price (5000 X 15.000) is 75,000. If the royalty rate is 10% of retail on hardcovers, your advance will be in the ballpark of $7500 (75,000 X .10).

As your books begin to sell, you will gradually earn out your advance. Once your sales have exceeded the amount of royalties covered by your advance, you'll begin to receive royalty checks. (Sadly, the majority of books never earn back their advance. However, the author is not expected to return it.)

It's customary for advances to be broken up. For example, 25% of the advance is paid upon signature of the contract, another 25% when the publisher approves the final manuscript, and 50% when the book is actually printed.

What amount should you expect? Well, offers for advances fluctuate so wildly that applying the law of averages becomes almost meaningless. If you stick your feet in a broiler oven and your head in a bag of ice, the average temperature will say you're comfortable—a misleading concept. Just so, a celebrity author could get a million dollar advance (extremely rare in the YA market), whereas authors who work with small presses might receive a grand or two—or no advance at all. That said, the "average" advance for a YA book by a new author is between five and fifteen thousand dollars.

New writers often ask why their royalties are such a small percentage of the eventual price of the book. "I wrote the book!" they protest. "Without me, the book wouldn't exist. If it sells for $6.50, shouldn't I get more than forty-five cents a copy?"

Here's why royalties are a little slice of the big cake. Publishers must cover all the following costs: editing, designing, cover art, printing, marketing, warehousing, sales staff and book expos, distribution—and author royalties. These add up to a hefty investment, which must all be paid out of 50% to 60% of the retail price of the book—because the retailer gets the other 40% to 50%.

Not only that, but publishers have the joy of participating in an industry-wide policy where a retailer can order as many copies as it wishes of a particular title from a publisher, and then if those copies don't sell, the books may be returned. The retailer owes nothing for unsold copies. (When "returning" paperbacks, retailers often don't return the books themselves. Instead, they rip off the front covers and send them back without the interiors, to save shipping. The books themselves end up in landfills because it's illegal to sell a book without its cover—for obvious reasons.)

Loads of books are returned. And the publisher absorbs the loss.

As for rights to your work, I'm not qualified to address this complex subject. I do know from experience that each time your book goes into a foreign country, you will receive a separate contract and a separate advance—unless your original publisher has bought world rights, in which case your foreign rights will be spelled out in the original contract and your foreign advance will be split with your main publisher. Your agent—if you have one—will fully understand the sale of your publishing rights, and negotiate the best terms possible for your situation. I also recommend getting your own copy of *The Writer's Legal Companion*, by Brad Bunnin and Peter Beren, which does a great job of covering the ins and outs of first rights, serial rights, foreign rights, copyrights, and other subjects of interest to writers.

Editing

Once you have a contract, the next step along your trek to fame and fortune (or notoriety within your family and a few extra bucks in the bank) is getting your book edited.

Depending on the size of your publishing company and the contract you have, you may wait a year or more before you enter the editing process. (Use the time to get started on your next novel.) When it's your turn in the rotation, your book will receive your editor's concentrated attention.

First, you'll receive an e-mail or have a conversation with your editor about revisions. For example, the first editor who worked on *The Seer and the Sword* sent a two page e-mail asking for additional exposition in a number of places. He'd noticed, for instance, that I left out a pivotal scene regarding the hero's capture. (Duh.)

Depending on your style, you may get notes asking for expansions, deletions, or both. If you tend to be lean, even skeletal with your prose, you'll be asked to flesh out scenes. If you're a wee bit wordy, you'll be asked to trim. (If you know a scene is redundant but you cherish it anyway because it's beautifully written, get ready to set aside your darling. If you can't take throwing scenes away outright, I recommend starting a file called Bits and Pieces, a file where you can keep your beloved passages and possibly use them somewhere else some other time.)

Editors will treat your manuscript the way a good mechanic treats your car, rooting around in the heart of the engine and pointing out what needs fixing. The diagnostic reports can be devastating—like when your whole book needs to be rewritten. But editors don't get to be where they are by accident. If they tell you something's flat or too full of air, odds are good they're right.

The editors I've had are some of the most dedicated and skilled people on earth. They've given me a big garage full of knowledge and handed me tools I didn't know existed. I've adored working with them. But I've met writers who didn't agree one bit with their editors, writers who thought editors were exerting too much control without understanding what the writer was trying to achieve. Sometimes editorial/authorial personalities and styles just don't mesh. When that happens, books suffer.

Think carefully before telling an editor he or she is completely wrong. Editors are trained to spot those telltale grease marks on your manuscript that indicate engine trouble within. They have a gift for you—the gift of objectivity. And they care about your book. They've staked their company's time, money, and reputation on you—an excellent reason to listen to what they have to say.

Editing may be tough and demanding, but editors do a lot more than edit. They handle many aspects of the business, from acquiring manuscripts (which means reading recommended manuscripts from agents and unsolicited submissions, if accepted) to preparing marketing plans for specific books. To find out more about all the jobs an editor covers, read *Agents, Editors, and You*, published by Writer's Market Library. This no-nonsense look at what goes on behind the scenes in publishing is eye-opening and highly educational.

Sad but true, an editor you're fond of may leave the publishing house that owns the rights to your book. This can turn into a setback for you because the editor who acquires your manuscript is the one who guides your book from prepublication to post printing. If he or she leaves, your book is "orphaned." The next editor assigned is unlikely to take the same interest and is probably overworked on behalf of other projects. Your book might not even be published after all. (Because unforeseen things happen in publishing—things such as editors leaving or companies going out of business, your contract will have a clause saying if the book isn't published within two to three years, all rights revert to you and the publisher has no more obligation.)

After you've completed revisions to the satisfaction of your editor, your book is ready for the next stage of the process. This is a major turning point in your career. Most book contracts specify delivery of an "acceptable" draft of your manuscript. You now have an editor approved draft, so you've fulfilled that clause. You're well on your way.

Line Editing and Copyediting

After you've completed broad revisions, an editor will go through and line edit your manuscript, looking for awkward turns of phrase, inconsistencies in characters, inaccurate statements, overused phrases, etc. Sometimes this editor is the same one who gave you the initial recommendations for revisions. Sometimes it's the copy editor.

Copy editors are trained in the fine points of grammar, among other things. They check through your book for correct spelling, punctuation, and word usage, as well as continuity. Copy editors are extremely meticulous and may catch things your literary editor missed.

After getting the comments from the copy editor, you'll go over your whole book again and rewrite as needed. By now, you may be getting just a tad sick of reading your novel. You'll have gone over it so many times you hardly see the words anymore. In some moods, you may even feel like the copy editor is a horrible quibbling nitpicker. So what if your two main characters have similar sounding names? So what if you used the word "clamor" too often? Who cares if there's a run-on sentence on page 129?

But again, copy editors know what they're doing. They're helping you polish your work, and they deserve a vote of thanks.

Funny story about something that was missed during copyediting: I once read a long book in which the male protagonist had the last name Pitt—and he was almost always referred to by his last name. The female lead was named Pat—and almost always referred to by her first name. Do you see where I'm going here? After several chapters of Pitt and Pat, I was chuckling during serious scenes. The book had an amazingly great plot so I finished reading it, but how strange to follow the adventures of Pitt and Pat.

If you sincerely disagree with a copy editor who wants you to remove phrases or paragraphs that you believe contribute something important to your novel, it's your call. You can refuse to go along with certain recommendations. I've sometimes disagreed with a copy editor, and it's no big deal. As the author, you have the final say. It's your story.

Cover Design

Meanwhile, your cover is being designed.

Despite the old saying "Don't judge a book by its cover," everybody does it and everybody will keep on doing it. Covers matter, because they get readers to pick up your book in the first place.

Editors who have been in the business for decades will tell you that when it comes to sales, a book's cover is more important than the book itself. Kind of a blow to us writers, but all too true. You've probably come across badly written books with fabulous covers that became best sellers. Or the opposite situation: wonderfully original and well-written books with dismal covers, dying an unsung death in the marketplace.

Important though the cover is, it's equally important for you as the author to understand up front that being a writer does not equal expertise in the area of book covers. To put it more bluntly, unless you're a renowned illustrator publishing a book on illustration, you won't be consulted about the cover art. Publishing companies have experts on hand who will give your book a cover designed to appeal to its audience.

If you have ideas for a cover, you're probably going to have to forget about them. The publisher chooses the artist, designer, and concept for your cover. Naturally, your publisher will hope you're happy with the result, but unless asked for your opinion, don't offer it. And depending on the size of your publisher, you might not even get a peek at your cover until it's a done deal.

Seeing your cover for the first time can be a magical feeling. When I saw what Trina Schart Hyman had painted for *The Seer and the Sword*, I got chills all over and then became flushed. Even though I'd never spoken to this artist, she had captured my characters perfectly. The same thing happened with the artwork of Christos Magganas, Greg Spalenka, and others.

Your cover represents your book to the world. The experts at your publishing house will do their best to brand your book with a look that's inviting, intriguing, and easily recognizable, a look that can be used repeatedly for future books you write.

Formatting and Design

Your novel will be formatted for printing. A design editor will decide font, type size, and layout.

Blurb Writing

Part of your book design includes a blurb—that enticing little teaser on the inside or back cover designed to appeal to browsing book buyers. People glance over the blurb before deciding whether to turn to page one.

A good blurb is crucial to a book's survival, but it's not normally written by the author. Professional blurb writers (often editors or assistant editors) are trained in the art of a quick pitch, and some of them have a real flair for it. Or sometimes the staff at a publishing house will select an excerpt from your book—a particularly exciting or mysterious passage—and use that as the teaser.

Personally, I'm happy to have help with the blurb because I find the idea of writing sales copy for my own work rather daunting. Some authors, however, are upset to find that a book they've labored over for years will rise or fall according to a small paragraph they neither wrote nor approved. Some have even had the unfortunate experience of discovering that their blurbs bear little relation to their books. But in the YA market, every book gets so much special care, you probably don't have to worry about that problem.

Galleys

You will receive a galley proof of your book, often referred to as "galleys." Galleys are pages showing your book in print format. The page size and formatting may be different from your final book. You may receive a hard copy, or the pages may be sent as a digital file that accepts comments and changes. Either way, you'll read through the galleys to catch any errors.

Even if you're well and truly fed up with your story at this stage, it's worth the effort to read through it with close concentration one more time. Every word. This is your last chance to make changes.

ARCs (Advance Reading Copies)

Advance reading copies (ARCs) are actual softbound books in the same format as the final book. They go out to reviewers, distributors, and sometimes book buyers. They are not for sale; they are for review. They're meant to spearhead your book, and give it a chance to have some presence in the marketplace before it's actually published.

Review copies usually go out three to six months in advance of the actual book. Sometimes ARCs have not yet been proofed and corrected. If so, they will say uncorrected proof right on the cover.

Positive reviews can make a big difference to your book, opening the way for schools and libraries to stock copies. This is vital for YA books. Teens and adults who like reading YA often find new titles by browsing library shelves. Friends recommend books to each other, and if those books are easy to find in a library, they stand a better chance of gathering a word-of-mouth following.

School Library Journal, Kirkus Reviews, and *Publishers Weekly* are nationally known publications that include reviews of new books for young adults. *Young Adult Library Services, Voice of Youth Advocates, The ALAN Review,* and *KLIATT* feature articles on how to promote teen literacy and serve the teen community. All of them have book reviews. Your publisher will try to secure reviews through such services.

Newspapers usually have a section for book reviews as well—a small section admittedly, but it's there. And some online communities offer wonderful review services written by teens themselves. The more reviews you can get, the better.

The Book

One fine day a box will be shipped to your residence. The box will contain copies of your finished book. Printed. Bound inside a cover. Wow. Few things in life can equal the bliss of holding your own bouncing book in your hand and knowing it now has a life of its own.

Time to celebrate. Throw a party. See if you can arrange a reading at your local bookstore. As you sign copies, revel in the culmination of all your effort and hope, persistence and patience, turmoil and uncertainty. You've done it! You're published!

Marketing

Hopefully before your first book signing, you've been introduced to the Marketing Beast. Better yet, you've formed a bond of sorts because whether you think of that beast as a beauty or a monster or both, and whether you want to pet it, shoot it, or run from it, it's going to play a big part in your career. Huge.

You want people to hear about your book. If they don't hear about it, they're unlikely to buy it and read it. You wrote the story, so you clearly believe in it. Now it's time to let others know it's out there ready to enlighten and entertain.

I grew up without a TV and saw very few movies. Books—and my own mind—were my entertainment. I loved books. Really really loved them. But that doesn't mean I had a single clue about marketing when my first book was published. At that time, I thought all books automatically appeared on bookshelves in bookstores. People bought them, and that was it.

Nothing could be further from the truth.

Marketing is expensive. Publishers cannot afford to put up the cash to make a splash with every title they print. They are likely to invest the most in books that are likely to sell the most.

I'm sorry to bring this up, but if you're serious about your career as an author, you may have to pump some of your own money and brain power into marketing.

If you're wondering where to start, there are some basic things you can do to help your publisher sell your books. One is to get an author website. Another is public speaking.

Author websites. Author websites have become almost essential. You want to have a presence on the web.

The norm for authors is to get your full name or pen name dot com. If the name is already taken, you can opt for dot net, dot org, or dot biz.

If you're web savvy and know how to design your own site, congratulations. If not, browse around for recommendations of people who know how to design and maintain sites. Your site should reflect your personality as a writer. It's a good idea to keep it updated, too. (I know that sounds like obvious advice, but some of my author friends and I have frequently forgotten to update when we get super busy with everything else.)

Public speaking. I've found speaking to be one of the best ways to generate interest in books. You can speak at local libraries, schools, writers' conferences, and other forums.

How do you let people know about you? Network. Be available. Let connections develop. Attend gatherings of authors and readers when you can. Talk to media specialists and let them know you're available for school programs. You might also try joining list serves that connect writers and readers. (A list serve is an e-mail group centered around a specific interest. E-mails sent to the list serve address by any member of the group are broadcast to every other member. When you join, you agree to abide by the rules of the group, which may include confidentiality. You can find groups by doing a search for "list serve" + "young adult" + "writer.")

Working with teens can be a lot of fun. By visiting high schools, middle schools and junior highs, you get a chance to meet your reading audience and interact.

If you're unsure about how school visits work, I recommend reading *Terrific Connections with Authors, Illustrators, and Storytellers: Real Space and Virtual Links*, by Toni Buzzeo and Jane Kurtz, an excellent reference.

"But," you say, "I'd rather dance with a tornado than speak in public." If you feel that way, you're not alone. Many writers are introverted by nature and/or have no experience with public speaking. So if you're a shy soul or you've never given a talk, you might want to start a course at Toastmasters. Now.

If, after practicing on a sympathetic audience your tongue still ties itself into uncooperative knots when you stand in front of a group, try building more of a presence on the Internet. Some schools will set up chat rooms for writers or do e-mail interviews. Blogs are also an increasingly popular way to build an audience.

One way or another, find a way to reach out to the public. With few exceptions, the days of scribbling alone in a garret are firmly in the past.

Large Press vs. Small Press

New writers sometimes assume the experience of getting published is similar whether the press is small or large.

Nope. I've worked with small, midsized, and large publishers now, so I know firsthand how different the dynamics are among them. These differences are worth knowing about.

My experience: I was first published in the United Kingdom, but that's a bit of a long story and won't really provide clear information you can run with. Instead I'll give the outline of my publishing experience in America.

In the U.S. I started with a midsized independent press called Holiday House, which published *The Seer and the Sword* in hardcover. Holiday House occupies one floor of a smallish (by Manhattan standards) office building in New York City. The owners and editorial staff take a personal interest in each and every book they publish—roughly fifty new titles per year. Holiday House has been in business for over seventy years, and has an excellent reputation for quality books for children and young adults, books that often end up receiving honors and awards. They market exclusively to libraries and schools.

The Seer and the Sword did exceptionally well in hardcover. After two and a half years it went to the Dell Laurel-Leaf division of Random House in paperback. (Holiday House does not customarily publish paperbacks.)

Well, the Random House offices are in a skyscraper right off Times Square. When I scheduled a visit with them, I walked from my hotel through a dizzying bustle of light and sound and well-dressed crowds—and missed the entrance at first because I was craning my neck at how high the building reached.

Imposing glass doors opened into an impressively lofty space, a lobby bigger than the apartment where I lived for years. At the far side of the lobby, behind a long counter, four employees checked appointments for all the people upstairs, and issued security badges for approved visitors.

After showing my I.D. and getting a badge, I passed through the security gates into a wide hallway. I grabbed an elevator to the 19th floor, a place honeycombed with offices filled with busy bees working hard to create buzz for thousands of books.

And Random House fills the whole building. Wow. I felt like a small drop of honey inside a humongous hive. Honey, yes. There's great sweetness in being part of an organization absolutely dedicated to books. The Random House editors were friendly and kind—book lovers, all. (Indeed, love of books unites small, medium, and large publishers.)

When I returned from New York, all the buildings in my town looked teensy. The air seemed immensely quiet. And, among other things, I found myself with a new perspective on how books are made and sold.

There's that word again: sold. Yes, we're going back for another look at marketing.

After *The Seer and the Sword* was released in paperback, I discovered something else about how marketing works.

I visited the Tattered Cover in Denver—one of the biggest bookstores in the world. It is a book lover's paradise, with floors and floors of shelves upon shelves of books. I went there to browse and, of course, ended up in the teen section. There I saw massive displays holding multiple copies of a few chosen books that were published by the large houses such as Random and Scholastic. No one walking into the teen section could have missed those displays—they rose up from the floor and dominated the view.

However, I had to hunt for my own book. Eventually I found a single copy tucked away with its spine out on a shelf stuffed with paperbacks by dozens of authors. I would have had to know about *The Seer and the Sword* in advance to buy it in that bookstore, unless I somehow happened upon it while browsing.

Even I, clueless and naïve, realized right away that the catchiest cover in the world cannot reach out to a reader when it's invisible, spine out on the shelf.

So then I looked for a book I admired by another author. It was nowhere to be found. I asked a clerk if the store carried it. After fiddling with the computer for a while he declared they didn't but offered to order it if I wished.

Hmmm.

I had known books were not treated equally. However, that experience brought home how wide the difference between one book and another can be.

Later, after fraternizing with other authors, I discovered it's common for writers to find their books spine out in a bookstore. It's even more common not to find them at all. Why? Because there's only so much shelf space.

If your book doesn't have a conspicuous place in bookstores nationwide, does it mean you're not a good writer? Of course not. Your book can receive many honors and still not be very visible. Getting a good spot on retail shelves is all about a complicated mix of sales pitches, name recognition, random chance, and other ingredients that defy analysis.

So how do you know if your book will get prominently displayed in retail outlets, multiple copies with the cover facing out, and other marketing treats?

You can get a pretty good idea by looking at the amount of your advance. A large advance—in excess of $100,000—means more risk to the publisher and more marketing for you. The bigger your advance, the more likely the publisher has decided your book has a good chance of making it onto the best-seller lists.

How do publishers make such decisions? Well, when they have a prolific author with a great track record, an author such as J.K. Rowling, Stephenie Meyer, or Lauren Myracle, an author with a groundswell of word-of-mouth, there's every reason to believe that an extra boost in marketing for that author will mean a boost in the bottom line for everyone—because it's likely to increase word-of-mouth even more.

But that doesn't mean every author who starts to develop a following will get a marketing boost. Many, many books are left to make it—or not—on their own. Statistics seem to support the idea that there's room for only a few authors to occupy the top spots in any given genre. Is this statistical wisdom true? I don't know. But at this point, it seems true enough that large publishers distribute their marketing budgets accordingly.

Then once in a while authors with no sales history at all are picked for stellar treatment. Maybe the publisher spots a niche in the market and gambles that a particular book, by filling that niche, can justify a big budget marketing plan. Maybe there's something about the author's life story that lends itself well to the creation of a marketing angle.

And if a writer has name recognition already—by being famous within popular culture—a publisher can capitalize on that. Instead of working to create new name recognition, they can draw attention to the fact that a celebrity has written a book. For example, when pop star Madonna entered the children's book market, her name was her passport to royal marketing. Her book had a first printing north of a million copies issued in dozens of translations. (Unknown writers who struggled for years to hone their craft, only to find their books would not receive attention, weren't very thrilled to see their sales overtaken by a celebrity's book. But large publishers argue that giant best sellers keep them solvent and able to publish unknown authors.)

Getting the picture? Most mega best sellers with sales in the millions are picked in advance by large publishers. Huge print runs must be ordered up front to keep pace with the marketing campaigns initiated for these books. A publisher doesn't want to be in the position of spending high dollars on marketing and then run out of books. And it's less expensive to print a million copies of one book than a hundred thousand copies of ten books. Once a million copies of a title are printed, it's imperative the publisher sell as many as possible. Thus the book will get lots of press. Reviews everywhere. Copies displayed on the shelves of not only bookstores nationwide but also big box chains offering a fairly small selection of books. The public will be made aware.

Publishers also have to contend with the utter unpredictability of the marketplace. Sometimes a book fails to sell even after heavy pushing. Readers just aren't captivated. No buzz. Big loss instead. What should have been a superstar turns into a black hole.

Then again, a book with a ten dollar marketing budget can come out of nowhere and shine, shine, shine. When that happens, publishers must scramble to order a big enough print run to fulfill the public's desire for copies, or lose sales.

To get back to the original point about guessing at your marketing budget based on the size of your advance: Is it good news for you if you get a large advance? Usually. However, a big advance for a book that turns out to be a sales flop can sink your career—because if a publisher puts a boatload of money into an advance for a book that flounders, the publisher is not going to buy your next book. (Thenceforth you may have to adopt a pen name.)

It's better to get a small advance and then earn it out than get a large advance and belly flop into the shallow end. If your advance is $5,000 but your book sells 50,000 copies, you're in a better position than the author whose advance is $500,000 but whose book sells "only" 300,000 copies. And before you feel jealous of big advances, remember that those authors who get picked for best-seller treatment do not necessarily have an easy time. The pressure to churn out top sellers is intense and can be hard to sustain.

And what about "midlist" books—books with respectable sales in the tens of thousands? They've come to resemble candles beside the floodlights of superstar bestsellers. Many midlist books are delightful—the sort you and I love to read (and write), but such books have often gone out of print within a year or two because their publishers can't justify the costs of continuing to print and warehouse them. They may be excellent novels but few people have heard of them and they don't have time to build a following.

The good news? Young adult novels are given more leeway in the marketplace. Unlike adult novels, which can live and die in the space of six months, YA books are allowed more time to find their way with readers. The rise of better digital printing technology is beginning to change the order of things, too. Books can be ordered on demand in small batches. Theoretically, this means there's no reason to take a book out of print.

How does all this information help you with your own book? Bottom line: unless your large publisher decides to put the money and energy into hyping your book—a rare occurrence—don't expect displays in stores or tours paid for by the publisher. You and your word-of-mouth cheering section will be picking up the slack. If you know all this in advance, you won't be shocked.

Enough of marketing. Beastly subject.

The advantages of working with a large press: distribution channels are well set up and maintained. Your publisher's name is known and respected. The staff is extremely capable—large houses attract some rattling good talent amongst editors, designers, and marketers. Your cover will probably be brilliant. And your novel will almost certainly be reviewed.

What About Small Presses?

The first time I visited Cottonwood Press—which has published the book you're now reading—I felt like I had entered Mary Poppins' bag. From the outside, the building doesn't look big enough to hold a successful publishing company that has been in business since 1986, a company with a reputation for quality and creativity.

Inside, the staff occupies windowed offices, sharing space with sunlight, colorful framed posters, computers, and books galore. In the back, a room packed with bookshelves serves as a shipping center.

A small press is to a big publishing house as a family is to a city. Everything is smaller and more personal, from start to finish.

To begin the process of submitting to a small press, look closely at its website. Assess whether your book would fit their existing catalog. If you've written a sunny tale, for instance, don't query Dark Horrors Press. If your story is contemporary YA fiction laced with profanity, don't approach a Christian publisher. If the title of your book is *Glorien, King of the Ripcloche Elves*, don't bother sending chapters to a press that publishes only historical fiction.

As of this writing, most small presses do not require agent representation before considering a manuscript. To approach a small press, follow the list in Chapter 5 on how to submit your work to agents. Instead of an agent you'll be submitting to an editor.

Respect the position of a small press editor, which is not the same as a large press editor. Like authors, small press editors are often juggling low budgets, high hopes, and overarching dreams. They're in love with the written word but their resources are limited. However much they might wish to, small press editors cannot promise you a big budget marketing plan.

Small publishers can't afford high numbers of returned books, so they look for niche markets, markets unlikely to send orders back. Some small presses market to libraries only, some to regional interests, some to educators, some to other specific groups. The definition of sales success is radically different than that of a large press. Whereas in a large press, sales of 150,000 copies may register as little more than a blip, in a small press 20,000 copies sold will be celebrated. Without the crushing pressure to manifest instant sales, your book will have more time to make a name for itself, and it's likely to stay in print longer.

There is a downside. Distribution channels aren't as wide. Pockets aren't nearly as deep. Advances are small—sometimes nonexistent—so you'll have to do tons of work before you have a hope of making money. And even if you're exceedingly popular within the niche of your small press, your sales won't ever hit the stratosphere. For one thing, a small press doesn't have the financial capability to order enormous print runs.

But working with a small press can be wonderfully rewarding—at least I think so. You'll have more access to the people connected with your book. Instead of one or two editorial meetings and then a sudden frantic rush to go through galleys, your editor will keep you posted about what's going on. Your book is one of only several printed in a year. You can work closely with the marketing department to find creative ways to get the word out on your title. No way are you going to fall through the cracks.

Depending upon the type of book you've written, your personality, ambitions, and ideals, you may be better served by a smaller house. If you want to be a superstar, a small press won't satisfy you, but if you're looking for modest success in a friendly atmosphere, you could be very happy with a small press. Also, if your title does well you'll have an excellent writing credit to add to your resume if you decide to pursue a larger publisher another time.

To find a small press that suits you and your work, go through *Writer's Market*, which has a section on small presses and what they're looking for. The majority publish nonfiction only, but between A and D I found five that publish fiction for young adults. You'll have to dig. And patience is required, because small presses publish a very short list of new books each year, so openings are scarce.

But when it works, it's great!

Interviews with Editors

This chapter on publishing wouldn't be complete without the editor's perspective. Next are interviews with four working editors who give their insights on what they look for from writers.

Cheryl Klein

Arthur A. Levine Books, an imprint of Scholastic, Inc.
www.cherylklein.com

Cheryl Klein is a senior editor at Arthur A. Levine Books, an imprint of Scholastic, Inc.

Is there something about the life of an editor that you wish more writers knew about or understood?

I know some writers appreciate this, but not all: Editors work a *lot*. We read probably 200+ manuscripts per year, make judgments on them, write sales copy and acquisition memos, work with our designers, present the books to our sales staff and create sales strategies, attend meetings, and somewhere in there actually edit the books—all of which takes time and thought and energy. Then we want to give our books under contract (which we love) our *best* time and thought and energy out of that—plus we want to have personal lives and fun as well! I'm routinely here till 7 o'clock at night on weekdays, and I usually work on Saturdays (and often Sundays too). So if I haven't gotten back to you, it isn't personal; it's that I'm trying to keep up with my workload and yet not get burned out altogether.

What are some of the most common mistakes writers make when writing YA? When sending in manuscripts?

When writing YA: They write what the trends are rather than their own story. Every publisher has been deluged with vampire manuscripts in the wake of the success of *Twilight* (just as wizard manuscripts went through a renaissance after *Harry Potter*). But what made those books successful was not just their entertaining plots—it

was the writer's ability to tap into the truth of teenage experience (forbidden love, wrestling with maturity and death) and represent that in an entertaining plot. Teens I think are really looking for truth more than anything else—some nugget of experience or reality that reflects their own lives or offers them guidance through the muddle of adolescence. If they find that, they'll hook into it.

When sending in manuscripts: Make sure the publisher actually publishes the kind of book you've written. I still remember the manuscript I opened as an editorial assistant, thinking it was another middle grade novel, only to discover in the first five pages that it was an adult erotic fantasy...

If you could suggest one thing that would help writers find success, what would it be?

Read. This is the most common advice out there, I know, but nothing is so useful in teaching good prose rhythms for your voice and familiarizing you with the genre you're working in—the better for you to put a stamp on it all your own.

Bella Pearson

David Fickling Books, an imprint of Random House

Bella Pearson is a senior editor with David Fickling Books, an imprint of Random House. She has worked for David Fickling Books since 2001; previously she completed an MA in children's literature at the Roehampton Institute and worked in an independent children's bookshop in London for many years. She lives in Oxford with her family.

Please note: David Fickling Books does not accept unsolicited queries.

Is there something about the life of an editor that you wish more writers knew about or understood?

There can be nothing more exciting in one's working life as an editor than a new manuscript fresh from the photocopier that on first read sends a shiver of excitement down the spine—as a result of the writing, the subject, originality, the pure quality of the author's work—whatever the reason might be. This sense of exhilaration and the potential discovery of a new talent is the main reason I do my job (although it can be quite a rare occurrence!). So perhaps the most important thing I wish that more writers understood about the life of an editor is that we really are on the same side. There are those who do all the work on their novel—the writers—and then those who do all the searching and reading and deciphering—and sometimes the twain really do meet. The satisfaction and excitement which comes as a result of publishing a fantastic novel from an extraordinary new writer, and sending it out into the big wide world to be read by as many people as possible, is the most thrilling feeling

of all, and should not be underestimated! And the more chances we have to do that as publishers, the better.

What are some of the most common mistakes writers make when writing YA? When sending in manuscripts?

Perhaps the most common mistake made by writers of children's literature as a whole is to talk down to their readership, and nowhere is this more evident than in the genre of teenage/YA fiction. This can be evident in many ways, but is particularly obvious in dialogue, where it can become apparent that the author is attempting to emulate the YA lingo of the time; or equally importantly, in subject matter, where sex, drugs and rock and roll can sometimes come way ahead of the most important thing: story.

Just like the rest of us, young adults read around their own lives, much more so than most adults; but many writers make the mistake of believing that they are interested in just a few restrictive, hormonally based things—which results in plenty of substandard issue-led novels. This is, of course, not to say that these issues are not essential in the lives of young adults—just that coming to terms with the adult world should not be seen as first and foremost more important than the integrity of the narrative.

On an entirely different note in answer to the second part of this question—first impressions really do count! Something as simple as reading a manuscript with double spacing can make all the difference—there is just so much on your desk that the easier to read, the better. If I receive a manuscript that has a straightforward and brief letter of introduction, and a clearly laid out text, then I am much more open and interested when it comes to reading and responding. If the manuscript has come from someone with professionalism, who is taking writing seriously, this can only help to endear them to the recipient who is peering around wobbly piles of manuscripts taller than themselves.

The bells and whistles that can come whirling through the postal service are more likely to make me think there must be something wrong with the writing itself if so much song and

Q&A

dance is necessary to draw attention to it. For instance, I once received a gift voucher, which of course I sent back. Bribery aside, I've gotten manuscripts accompanied by multicolored paper packaging and childlike bubble writing; photos of all the family and pets; one of the cleverest (and most dishonest!) times, someone sent in their book with a postcard claiming to be from a sales rep who knew me, proclaiming the book's popularity with readers.

If you could suggest one thing that would help writers find success, what would it be?

Just one thing...what a tricky question! My initial thought, though it seems such an obvious one, is the not-so-easy job of finding an agent. The sheer load of manuscripts that an editor receives means that those which come in recommended by an agent, particularly a well-respected agent, do get seen first. And this sense that the novel has already been spotted by someone else is very encouraging.

But if we are talking about individual characteristics, determination is one that springs to mind—the life of a writer is a hard one and can be a lonely one, so a great deal of strength is needed to keep going and remain hopeful. As in everything, tastes and likes vary tremendously from editor to editor—and although I'd like to think that I and every editor are absolutely open to all sorts of material, inevitably some part of the decision making process will be down to the sort of thing we personally enjoy. So if one individual rejects a book, this is not the kiss of doom; the ability to brush off the rejection and continue believing in your work is essential in order to find the right publisher.

Laura Backes

Editor of a variety of publications

Laura Backes has been part of the publishing field since 1986. She's worked at some of New York's top publishing houses in publicity (Ballantine Books) and subsidiary rights (Farrar, Straus & Giroux), as a literary agent (Goodman Associates and later with The Backes Agency), and as a freelance editor for small presses and self-published authors. Since 1990 Laura has helped educate countless aspiring authors on the craft of writing for children as publisher of Children's Book Insider: The Newsletter for Children's Writers (see www.write4kids.com for more information). In October 2000, Laura formed Children's Authors' Bootcamp, an intensive two-day workshop on writing fiction for children, which she teaches throughout the country with author Linda Arms White (see www.WeMakeWriters.com for more information). Laura is also the author of Best Books for Kids Who (Think They) Hate to Read (Prima Publishing/Random House), technical editor for Writing Children's Books for Dummies (Wiley) and has had articles on writing published in Writer's Digest and The Writer magazines.

Is there something about the life of an editor that you wish more writers knew about or understood?

I think writers commonly have two misconceptions about editors. One, they think editors sit around their offices all day reading. And because they envision editors ensconced in armchairs, reading with a cup of tea and a scone at their side, they wonder why editors

 can't take the time to personally respond to every submission. Or why editors complain when people send them inappropriate submissions (fiction when the publisher only does nonfiction, picture books when the editor specifically asks for novels, etc.) In reality, editors spend their days in meetings, editing manuscripts already under contract, negotiating new contracts with authors or agents, preparing reports for the sales and marketing departments, and going to more meetings. The reading is almost always done in an editor's spare time. So it's important that authors not waste that precious time with unprofessional submissions.

Two, many authors think editors go through the slush pile looking to reject as many manuscripts as possible. But every editor I know who reads unsolicited submissions does so because she's an eternal optimist. She desperately wants to find new writers to publish. Even if an editor works with a list of famous, established authors, she still needs to constantly find new blood. And nurturing a new talent is one of the joys of the job.

What are some of the most common mistakes writers make when writing YA?

I think many writers misunderstand what makes a young adult novel these days. I've been critiquing manuscripts for writers for 18 years, and very often when someone sends me a YA novel, it's really a middle grade book with a fifteen-year-old protagonist. In young adult books, the main character comes face-to-face with an adult situation for the first time, and absolutely must deal with it. At the end of the book, that character is no longer a child. The protagonist has grown up either mentally, physically, spiritually, emotionally, or all of the above. He's lost a certain amount of innocence and naiveté, and is better able to take on the real world. Not everything he learns is necessarily pleasant, because reality can be bittersweet, but the main character is now facing the situations from the plot with eyes that weren't completely open before the book began.

Many YA manuscripts don't have that edge to them. They're about finding a date for the prom, or getting in with the popular crowd. Those situations can certainly occur in a YA novel, but they would be part of a larger, more substantial story.

Another mistake some writers make is not including any sub-plots. Young adult novels are as richly layered as novels for adults. The main plot line must be reinforced by related sub-plots that explore the protagonist's relationship with other characters, or delve into connecting aspects of the protagonist's life that shed light on how to deal with the story's conflict. Juggling all these threads takes skill, but when done well, the experience for the reader is much more rewarding. Chris Crutcher is one YA author who is very adept at developing several complex sub-plots and somehow bringing them all together at the end.

If you could suggest one thing that would help writers find success, what would it be?

You'll always hear editors tell aspiring writers to read, read, read, and it's such important advice that I'm going to give it as well. That said, I think another element to success in the YA market is developing your own unique voice. In YA more than any other age group, an author can hold the reader's attention on the power of voice alone. Many novels are written in first person and center around the narrator's inner struggles. If they're created with a strong, original, convincing voice, the reader will feel like the narrator's best friend. A writer's voice takes a while to emerge, so be patient. Don't rush it. Get to know your main character and try writing short essays in her voice every day. Allow your character to be flawed as well as fabulous. Urge her to talk about anything and everything that's important to her, even if you don't plan on using the information in your book. You want to disappear into your character, and at the same time you want your character to come alive. It can be a little scary—losing yourself to your story—but that's how the best books come to be.

Q&A

Cheryl Miller Thurston

Cottonwood Press, Inc.

Cheryl Miller Thurston is a writer who founded her own publishing company in 1986. Cottonwood Press, Inc., is a niche publisher focusing primarily on books to help middle school and high school English and language arts teachers. It also publishes books related to the field of writing and to education in general. Thurston edits all books published by the small company.

Is there something about the life of a small press editor that you wish more writers knew about or understood?

Small publishers—perhaps even more than large publishers—really, really do want to find manuscripts that work for us. Truly. We need to keep replenishing our list with good books that are a good fit. We don't approach the slush pile as the enemy. We approach it with anticipation—maybe one of these manuscripts is going to be just what we need! If a writer sends me a query that tweaks my interest in any way at all, I take a chance and ask to see the whole work. I'm always hoping for a gem.

What are some of the most common mistakes writers make submitting books for consideration to a small press?

The biggest mistake they make is not doing their homework. However, I doubt that this mistake is limited to submissions to small presses.

Around half of the manuscripts I receive are wildly inappropriate for us. We receive a lot of manuscripts for picture books for tod-

EDITOR Q&A

dlers. We don't publish picture books, and we don't publish books for toddlers. Our primary focus is materials for teachers to use with middle school and high school kids.

We receive crazy things every now and then. Just a few examples: a book of tattoo designs, instructions for making choir robes, gushing poetry clearly not appropriate for kids, a nonfiction manuscript purporting to explain why the theory of relativity cannot possibly represent reality, and the biography of a stalker.

Now, really. Does anyone go to our website filled with materials for the language arts classroom and think, "Ah! My stalker bio will fit perfectly here!"?

No. Such writers are not doing even the most basic homework. Everyone, and I mean everyone, who submits to a small press should spend at least a minute or two at the publisher's website. Even a short look around will give a sense of what the company is about. If it features babies and toddlers, don't send a book about your experiences in the Vietnam War. If it's filled with serious academic titles, don't send your proposal for "Granny's Llama and the Humpity Dumpity Camel."

Another mistake: spending a lot of time on the manuscript and not a lot of time on the cover letter. I often have the feeling that the cover letter was dashed off in a flash, without even a proofread. I'm not a big meanie eager to strike down a writer for the smallest "it's/its" mistake. Heck, I've made the same mistake. But when a cover letter is filled with spelling and grammatical errors, I know that the writer is very unlikely to have submitted a manuscript worth looking at. Experience has proven that—always—to be the case, and I don't take much of a second look.

When a writer who is careful about her craft submits a well-written cover letter, I know instantly that she knows what she's doing. The cover letter makes it abundantly clear.

Cover letters really, really matter—at least to me.

I think I should mention one more thing. I really hate getting materials from writers who are so afraid their ideas will be stolen that they send only a couple of pages of their manuscript. Still,

they expect you to offer them a publishing contract. That's a real sign of an amateur.

If you could suggest one thing that would help writers find success, what would it be?

May I please suggest *two* things?

First, don't do what I sometimes did, before I knew better, when I was working as a freelance writer. That's what I call the *scattershot* mailing.

I would write a piece on, say, an experience I had as a teacher, reaching a seventh grader through his love of cats. The specific magazine I had in mind for the piece would reject it, and then I would go through *Writer's Market* and select magazines I knew nothing about but which looked like they *might* take something like my piece. Maybe a magazine on pets. Or a magazine on educational software. Or a journal for pet store owners. I knew nothing about these magazines, *nothing,* yet I had the wild hope that something about my piece would just capture their fancy. I would send it out to all of them.

It would be rejected by all of them. The scattershot approach never worked. Not once. Crafting my prose to fit a magazine I had studied *did* work.

Second, if you're serious about having your work published by a certain publisher, read books that the company publishes. Read as many of them as you can. Understand what appeals to the editors by reading what appeals to them.

Years ago, I received a large manuscript that astounded me. The author, Randy Larson, clearly knew, really *knew,* what Cottonwood Press is all about. He had used our books in his classroom, and he spoke knowledgeably of them in his cover letter. He wrote a book that was so "us" that I snapped it up immediately. And, though *Hot Fudge Monday* has been in print for 12 years, it remains one of our best-selling books, ever. The man had done his homework.

* * * * *

Your Publishing Journey

Holding your published novel in your hands is quite a feeling. I'm still astonished when I look at my own books and realize that years of dreaming, thinking, working, and believing have become visible in a bound volume with a beginning, middle, and end.

Just as the old proverb says, a journey of a thousand miles begins with a single step. As you find your way along your own path to publishing, enjoy the hike!

CHAPTER SEVEN

SELF-PUBLISHING *your* Book

SELF-PUBLISHING *your* BOOK

I'll admit that once upon a time I was a snob about self-publishing. Back then I believed it was the ultimate hubris for a self-published writer to call him/herself an author. Self-published books seemed to be popping up every time I turned around, and I thought of them as wasted trees sacrificed to the egos of those unable to accept that they couldn't write well enough to find a "real" publisher.

My prejudice was not unfounded. I've seen self-published books written at the level of "roses are red, violets are blue,"—only without the roses or violets. They stink.

Okay, so that's the bad side.

There's another side though, and it's won my respect.

Sometimes dedicated, talented, skilled writers can't get published the traditional way. These writers have tried and tried to get the attention of an agent or editor without success. Maybe they don't write the sort of fiction that's hot today, or the market they write for is very small. Maybe they're on the cutting edge of written art, creating a whole new style an editor may love but won't take a chance on. And maybe the luck of the draw just hasn't favored them. Whatever the reason, they've written good books and can't get published.

Self-publishing can perform a rescue.

Let's look at a few of the advantages and disadvantages of self-publishing.

Advantages
- You won't have to wait years until your book is available in print. Whereas traditional publishers have a tight rotation of books scheduled years in advance, self-publishing can happen in a matter of weeks after the book is

written. If it's important to you to give your teenage son or niece or friend a book you've created—and before that person is thirty-five—this can be quite a motivating factor.

- You won't have to worry about submitting and being rejected, submitting and being rejected, submitting...
- You'll be in charge of your own work from beginning to end.
- If your book sells well, you get to keep all the profits.

Disadvantages

- Because the only screening process necessary for a book to be self-published is the writer's wallet, plenty of self-published books are terrible. You will, therefore, have to find a way to set your work apart if you want to create a market for it.
- You won't have the advice and guidance of a professional editor, unless you hire someone. The person you hire might not have the expertise of someone working directly with current titles in an active marketplace.
- Your book is unlikely to appear in retail stores. Distribution channels for self-published books are lousy. Traditional review services do not accept self-pub titles—if they did, they'd soon drown in the deluge. Tens of thousands of books are self-published every year.
- You'll have to pay for everything, and you may not recover your initial investment. This is fine if your ambition is not about cash.
- You'll be in charge of your own marketing plan. Without established distribution channels, this is much tougher than most people anticipate. You'll have to go out and find your audience.

As a self-publisher, you can oversee all steps of the publishing process yourself, hiring help as needed as you prepare your book for print and then decide on a printer and a print quantity. However, you should definitely do some research first. Informed people tell me that two "bibles" of the self-publishing industry are *The Self-Publishing Manual*, by Dan Poynter, and *The Complete Guide to Self-Publishing*, by Tom and Marilyn Ross. Reading these books may help avoid costly mistakes.

Print on demand. In the past, publishers and self-publishers had to agree to fairly large print runs in order to get a reasonably priced book. (The larger the print run, the lower the price per book.) Printing just a few copies of a book was simply not cost effective. Now, however, print on demand (POD) technology allows you to order or "demand" small quantities of books as you need them. POD has caused many changes in the world of publishing, and those changes are still taking place, rapidly.

Many companies provide POD services, but there are important differences between them. Some simply provide printing services. Some try to present themselves as a form of traditional publishing and persuade writers they've landed traditional contracts when signing up. (Traditional publishing companies don't charge *you* when they agree to publish your book.) It is very important to research your options carefully and to know exactly what you are getting into before you sign on with a POD publisher. You may be able to find something that suits your situation perfectly, but please proceed with caution.

Interviews with Self-Published Writers

Still wondering whether self-publishing would suit you? Here's something else to put into the mix. Following are interviews with self-published authors who have agreed to share their experience and expertise with you.

Q&A

Becky Clark Cornwell

Ampersand Press
www.beckyclark.net

Published book:

An UnCivil War–The Boys Who Were Left Behind

Why did you decide to self-publish?

My son was born a voracious reader and in about third or fourth grade he was reading his sister's *American Girl* books. But they were girlie and he was embarrassed. He really enjoyed the historical fiction genre so he and I trekked to the library where I assured him he could find a treasure trove of "boy" historical fiction. Not so. The librarians and I could only come up with a handful of books that fit the bill, most of which he'd already read.

As we were walking to our car he said, "Why don't you just write one, Mom?"

After I guffawed at this twitchy gauntlet he threw at my feet, I went home, dug out a yellow legal pad, and started watching the Broncos game. Before halftime, there were four full pages of periods of history I'd be interested in writing about.

By the end of the game, I had narrowed my list down to the Civil War because I knew that in our school district they studied the Civil War in 5th grade, the target market I wanted to aim at. I am, first and foremost, a practical writer. Not simply "what am I passionate about" but also "what am I passionate about that has a ready-made market."

I read about a local conference about self-publishing, put on by the Colorado Independent Publishers Association. So I went, and lots of very smart, generous people made me believe I could do it and it would be easy. Ha!

What are the advantages/rewards of self-publishing?

Speed, for one. If you're talented, you can write, edit and produce a good book within a year. Dealing with traditional publishers, large or small, can be as slow as a turtle on Valium. Also, all the money from a book sale goes straight to my bottom line. I was at a big book signing with a famous author. He watched in amazement as I stuffed ten dollar bills right into my pocket (the lion's share of which was pure carnivorous profit). For every book he signed, he got only eighteen cents. Which he never actually saw for six months. (Of course, when he got his six month royalty statement, it had lots more money on it than what I had wadded up in my pocket over a six month period.) And I love the autonomy of it all. I can do whatever I want to promote or distribute my book. All the risk is mine, but so is all the reward.

What are the disadvantages/trials?

Self-publishing is like getting a PhD in every aspect of book publishing while sitting on a lighted Roman candle. My biggest problem has been distribution. Grab a hankie and listen to my sad story. Three thousand copies of *An UnCivil War* were delivered to me in August 2001. Remember what happened in September? Yeah. My marketing plan was all about mailing free copies to reviewers and distributors, but no one was accepting any mail because it might be tainted with anthrax. I had to totally regroup and rethink my plan, which got scaled back to within an inch of its life.

So, I've sold those 3000 copies in lots of weirdly fun ways, none of which I envisioned when I started. Mostly I sell books at book signings during conferences for teachers and librarians, at school visits, or at events for home educators. But I've sold books standing in line at the post office when someone asked about the ten identical envelopes I was mailing. Another time a teenager was loading my groceries into my car and asked what was in the big box that was in his way. I sold a book to him, too.

The other disadvantage is that it's exhausting doing everything yourself. My humble little business venture is easy compared to many, and I have the luxury of not having to work a day job. But

still, I've found that I can either write and create or I can handle business. I can't seem to do both consistently, even though I'm a fairly organized, self-disciplined gal. I find it easier—and certainly more fun—to write than to deal with book production or fulfillment or updating www.BeckyClark.net.

What have you learned about marketing?

I'm one of the rare writers who loves marketing. I already had a solid foundation in it because my husband and I have owned a successful small business since 1994 and it was always my job to do the marketing and promotion. I'm a good schmoozer, I like meeting people, and I'm always happy to talk about myself and my book or writing and publishing. I read a lot of books about marketing too, especially book promotion.

What has surprised you the most about self-publishing?

I guess the most surprising thing to me was how hard it was to land distributors to get my book into bookstores and libraries. And I hear it's even harder now. Just as I was getting into the Wunnerful World of Publishing, most of the big distributors redefined their terms and wanted the publishers they dealt with to have more than a handful of titles. I didn't try too terribly hard, however, because once I rethunk my marketing plan, I was having success and lots of fun *and* I was able to stick those ten dollar bills in my pocket.

Now it's easier to find distribution in nontraditional channels via the Internet, but that's an increasingly noisy and crowded marketplace. You need to create some serious buzz to get noticed.

Are you seeking publication through traditional publishers? If so, why?

Yes. I have decided to travel the more traditional path right now. The stuff I love to do—writing, creating, marketing—I can still do, but the stuff I'm not wild about—production, fulfillment, distribution—would be handled by others who, ideally, would be better at it. I guess I also want that corporate pat on

the head, too. The one that says I'm officially good enough for the big league. Realistically, anybody with a couple of thousand-dollar coins to rub together can self-publish a book. But getting noticed by a literary agent or a big deal editor is as hard as tap dancing in a swamp. At this stage in my writing career I'd like that validation. Don't get me wrong—I've received lots of enthusiastic e-mails from kids and adults telling me they like my book—several in the category of "You Changed My Life" or "I Never Liked To Read Until I Read Your Book," which can reduce any author to a puddle of gooey ego. But to be anointed by a company like Random House or Simon and Schuster would, to me, be the delicious flag planted at the top of Mount Publishing.

I have felt successful every step of my self-publishing journey—when I finished the manuscript, when I first held my beautiful, tangible biblio-baby in my hands, when I got my first rave review (and all the subsequent ones!)—the list is long. But now I want a different kind of publishing success. It's not any easier or any more lucrative, just different.

What's the most important advice you have for people considering self-publishing?

Do your homework. Know what you're getting into. Seek out people and organizations to help you in your journey. Understand that writing is rewriting and publishing is marketing. Hire an excellent editor who will do everything from checking your commas to seeing your manuscript as a whole. Spend money for a gorgeous, eye-catching cover and spine. If you're writing for kids, know kids. Your father/mother/spouse/child/neighbor/dental hygienist is not your critique partner—find lots of people who don't love you to tell you the truth about your writing. Get an ISBN. Barcode your book. Don't let anything about your book look like you did it yourself. Solicit competitive bids for everything. Check references. Practice safe accounting. Embrace Becky's Rule Of At Least Two: Do at least two marketing things every day, add at least two names to your database, and write for at least two hours.

Q&A

Pat McFadden

Green Turtle Press
www.greenturtlepress.com

Published book:

Turtle Island

Why did you decide to self-publish?

In 2000, I had a manuscript that won a contest at the Pikes Peak Writers conference. I thought that was a shoo-in for getting it published, and did have a small publisher who was interested in it. However, they couldn't offer advances, and the editor said they had other books in the works and wouldn't be able to get mine out for four or five years. Well, I wanted to start doing the author visit circuit, and for that you need books, right? I'm a very hands-on, do-it-myself kind of person—I sew and garden and make jam and beeswax candles and homeschooled my kids and have owned a couple of businesses (a preschool and an herb shop)—so it didn't seem all that daunting to me to publish my own books. So I did. The publishing part was easy. The selling part still has me a little stumped.

What are the advantages/rewards of self-publishing?

You get to make all the decisions from what kind of paper to use to what the cover will look like. For me, it was also fun to get to know about all the ins and outs of the printing process. I learned to use Pagemaker and did my own typesetting, though I did get two other people to edit the final draft. (This is an absolute must. There were still errors, but a lot fewer than there would have been if I'd done my own editing.) Self-publishing is *fast*. I had 2000 books in my garage

within four months of deciding to self-publish, and it can be done even faster. It can be lucrative, if you are a good salesperson, since you get to keep a higher percentage of the book price.

What are the disadvantages/trials?

Some 1400 of those 2000 books may still be sitting in your garage six years later if you didn't really get out there and sell, sell, sell. You have no marketing department—you are your marketing department—and distribution can be very tricky. Also, many people have the attitude that you had to self-publish because your work wasn't good enough to be published "for real." Sadly, that is sometimes true, but I don't think that the percentage of schlocky self-published books is any higher than what is cranked out by the trade publishers. I mean, have you read some of the celebrity books that are out there? Please!

What have you learned about marketing?

I've learned that it's not for the faint of heart. It takes a lot of hard work and self-confidence to get out there and sell your wares. The self-publishers I know who are successful spend a huge amount of time going to all sorts of venues such as schools, libraries, teachers' conferences, book clubs and anywhere else that people who read can be found. To paraphrase: "Wherever two or more are gathered talking books, there are you."

What has surprised you the most about self-publishing?

One of the best surprises is that there is a huge and supportive network of independent and small publishers who are more than happy to help their fellow entrepreneurs out. (Such publishers generally prefer the terms "independent publisher" or "small publisher" over "self-publisher.") I belong to the Colorado Independent Publishers Association and used to belong to the Small Publishers Association of North America. They both give conferences and workshops on all aspects of the business and are great for making contacts of all sorts.

Are you seeking publication through traditional publishers? If so, why?

Yes. All the time. I have a picture book coming out in the spring with Starbright Books and am circulating manuscripts for everything from baby poetry to a YA historical novel. My time is limited and I'd rather focus on writing and let someone else worry about the publishing details. Which doesn't mean I won't put my publisher hat on again someday.

What's the most important advice you have for people considering self-publishing?

Consider *very* carefully. Do you like to have a lot of control? Can you afford to wait a long time to earn back your initial investment? Can you afford to never earn it back? Is your book really ready to be seen in print? How do you know? (I used a POD publisher for my first book, sold about a hundred copies and asked for feedback before setting up my own imprint.) How much time and effort can you realistically put into it, and are you willing to do so? These are all good questions to ask yourself before embarking on any big commitment, but especially self-publishing. If you don't want to take a long voyage, don't get on the boat.

Q&A

Teresa R. Funke

Bailiwick Press
www.teresafunke.com

Published books:

Remember Wake
Dancing in Combat Boots
Doing My Part

Why did you decide to self-publish?

When I decided to self-publish back in 2001, I was no stranger to publishing, having sold dozens of articles, short stories and personal essays to literary and commercial magazines and run a freelance writing business for ten years.

There are many reasons people decide to self-publish. For some it's a matter of maintaining control over their work. For others it's about timing; they need the book to be available sooner than the publishing industry's typical turnaround of 18–36 months. For others it's because they tried the traditional houses first and were turned down so they decided to go it on their own. For still others, it's the spirit of the entrepreneur that drives them, the desire to do it all themselves. For me, it was all of those things.

I'd initially tried to submit my first book, *Remember Wake*—a historical novel—to traditional publishers. I even had an agent. But the agent had the manuscript for several months and then promptly retired from the business. A few editors had asked to see the book, but sat on it for months at a time before rejecting it. An editor once told me *Remember Wake* was so good she couldn't put it down, yet she still decided not to publish it. I found that totally perplexing.

SELF-PUBLISHER Q&A

Meanwhile, during the two and a half years that I was submitting the book, the people on whom the novel was based—people connected to Wake Island in World War II—were starting to pass away. Suddenly it became more important to me to get the book published and into the hands of the remaining survivors than it did to get that big, New York contract. So I contacted a print on demand company and, within a few months, I had a printed book to sell or give away.

I had assumed I would continue to submit *Remember Wake* to traditional publishers, but I never did. I got caught up by that entrepreneurial spirit and the desire to see if I could make the book a success on my own, which I accomplished. My second book, *Dancing in Combat Boots*, was also turned down by several top agents who told me they admired the book, but weren't convinced a short story collection would sell well. So my writing partner, Karla Oceanak, and I started Bailiwick Press and we published that book ourselves, enjoying every step in the process. We also produced my middle grade novel, *Doing My Part*, and made it the first in my Home-Front Heroes collection. We worked incredibly hard over the next six months getting those two new books to press and reissuing *Remember Wake*, but we were extremely proud of the results. And now when people tell me they love my books, it feels maybe even a little better than if I'd had a major publisher because my partner and I did it all ourselves.

What are the advantages/rewards of self-publishing?

Advantages include being able to produce the books you want without having to make changes to suit a publisher's idea of the marketplace. You can make more money off the sale of each book than a traditional royalty would give. You have a say in the cover design, something most traditionally published authors are not allowed. Many authors come to self-publishing after seeing one of their traditionally published books virtually ignored by their publisher. And no one can sell your book better

than you, because no one will care about it the way you do. I'm also able to roll with the changes in the market, too. For example, I'd written *Remember Wake* for adults, and not until later did I figure out that teenagers were finding and loving the book. Then I was able to shift some of my marketing focus to include them. I'm thrilled that they enjoy it.

What are the disadvantages/trials?

Self-publishing is most definitely not for everyone. Whereas most traditionally published writers have the luxury of spending much of their work time on their writing (and the occasional book signing or school visit, etc.), self-published writers spend countless hours on layout and design, promotion, distribution, tracking inventory, dealing with buyers, etc. It takes a special kind of person to make it big in self-publishing, someone who is interested in all aspects of the business and is willing to work very hard.

What have you learned about marketing?

I'm not gonna lie to you. Marketing self-published fiction can be an uphill battle. Whereas self-published nonfiction books can sell very well based on the credentials of their authors or on the subject matter of the book, fiction is subjective, and many people aren't willing to take a risk on a self-published novel that may or may not be good. The first thing you must do for your book is have it professionally edited. And make sure your back-of-the-book blurb is so compelling any kid picking it up will simply have to open it. If you haven't produced a well-written, well-edited book, no amount of marketing savvy will save you.

Once your book has been edited and you've identified your target market, you're ready to take the first step on that uphill journey. When you reach an obstacle, go around it. Many book reviewers, for example, won't touch self-published fiction, so forget about them. Suggest a feature article to your newspaper instead. Many bookstores won't carry self-published fiction, so

don't waste your time trying to convince them otherwise. Go around the bookstores and find a way to reach your target markets directly. With teens, that often means using the Internet. Send organizations a sample copy to peruse and endorsements for the book; create a compelling talk that they'll just have to hear. Oh, and get yourself a website, especially if you're writing for teens.

The biggest challenge in self-publishing, especially with fiction, is finding ways to spread the word about your book. But if you can embrace the process, if you can think of marketing as a creative endeavor, you'll be amazed at the clever ways you can come up with to promote your book.

What has surprised you most about self-publishing?

How much work it really is. Before I self-published, I joined an organization called Colorado Independent Publishers Association and it was the best thing I ever did. Through them, I learned everything I needed to know to get started, but I also got a taste of what lay before me. These were some of the most committed authors I'd ever met. They cared passionately about their writing and were willing to work their butts off to see their books succeed. It was inspiring and a little intimidating just to be around them.

Are you seeking publication through traditional publishers? If so, why?

I'm happy with my current endeavors, but my goal has always been to get my books and my message out to as many readers as I can. All of my books are based on interviews with real people and I consider that a sacred trust, one that adds value to our world. It's a joy to me to create fictional characters based on the life experiences of actual people. As long as I feel I'm able to help get those stories out there, I'm happy to do it myself. If the time ever comes that I feel a bigger publisher could handle that task better, I would consider turning it over. We have finally

reached a point in the history of publishing where it's not an all or nothing situation. We can have the best of both worlds depending on our goals for our individual projects. It's an exciting time.

What's the most important advice you have for people considering self-publishing?

Consider your goals for your book. If you want to see your book in every bookstore in America, if you want to try to sell 100,000 copies, then try the traditional publishers first. If they don't pick up your book, but you still feel it's worth publishing, do it yourself. If the whole concept of self-publishing appeals to you from the start, then do it and do it right. Read books on how to self-publish, attend talks and seminars, join self-publishing organizations or submit to their newsletters, and most importantly, talk to other self-pub authors. Keep your goals realistic and your hopes high. Oh, and don't order five thousand copies on your first print run, especially with fiction. Please trust me on this one. Start with one thousand. If they sell out, great! Order more. There's nothing more depressing than a garage full of unsold books. And there's nothing more satisfying than saying, "Guess I need to do a second printing." Or a third, or a fourth . . .

What's the next step in your writing journey?

Karla and I have decided to go beyond what most self-published authors do. We started our own press, Bailiwick Press, with the intention of not just publishing our own work, but the works of others in the upcoming years. Bailiwick means something that you're good at, something that is your passion. Our passion is books. Our motto for Bailiwick is "Books With Something to Say," and that's what we're looking for, books that are important, that have a good message encased in an entertaining read, that teach young readers something about their world in a way that doesn't feel like learning, that appeal to those reluctant readers out there, and that can be beautifully packaged and designed.

 And we'll be looking for a new breed of author, someone who is willing to get involved in making his/her own book a success, someone who is willing to work with teachers and educators to reach kids in new ways. If small publishing houses are going to compete against the giants, we have to stand out, we have to be different and daring and good. We have to offer something the bigger houses don't. And as well as readers, we'll be serving writers through a variety of products geared toward helping new writers. Because writing can be and should be a lifelong interest, and no matter where you are in your writing journey, you should be able to easily find the support you need. That's what makes this a new age for writers. With the influence of the Internet, it's not just going to be the writer with the big, New York contract who makes a splash anymore; it's going to be that writer next door who just happens to say what we all need to hear.

CHAPTER EIGHT

WORDS *of* WISDOM *from* AUTHORS

WORDS *of* WISDOM *from* AUTHORS

SURE, IT'S SIMPLE, WRITING FOR KIDS...
JUST AS SIMPLE AS BRINGING THEM UP.
  – URSULA K. LEGUIN

On the following pages are interviews with authors of young adult fiction who are writing and publishing today. They answer questions about what's involved with subgenres, dealing with rejection, and various approaches to finishing a book. Then they delve into the rewards of being a writer.

Q&A

T.A. Barron

www.tabarron.com

Published books:

The Great Tree of Avalon trilogy
> Book I: *Child of the Dark Prophecy*
> Book II: *Shadows on the Stars*
> Book III: *The Eternal Flame*

The Lost Years of Merlin epic
> Book I: *The Lost Years of Merlin*
> Book II: *The Seven Songs of Merlin*
> Book III: *The Fires of Merlin*
> Book IV: *The Mirror of Merlin*
> Book V: *The Wings of Merlin*

The Adventures of Kate trilogy:
> *Heartlight*
> *The Ancient One*
> *The Merlin Effect*

Also picture books, nature books, and other books (See website).

Please say a few words about the YA subgenre in which you write.

I write books I would like to read. That means each story must have four essential elements—a character I care about, a magical place, a gripping dilemma, and a compelling idea. With those four elements in place, I can feel sure that the reader—and myself—will have an enjoyable journey. And so I like a story where an individual must deal with personal issues as well as overarching issues. The

mythic quest—call it fantasy if you prefer—allows me to incorporate all of these qualities.

The realm of fantasy gives me a great opportunity to wrestle with some of life's biggest questions in the context of a good old-fashioned page-turner. For example, telling the story of Merlin's lost years allowed me to explore the idea that all of us have a magical person hidden down inside of ourselves. Just like that unknown boy who washed ashore, each of us has the potential to reach for the stars.

Fantasy allows me to bend the rules of our existence—highlighting troubling issues of our time. In a way, this kind of story is like a bent mirror. I can write about life with more intricacy and power—bending the rules of our world—in order to emphasize certain elements and de-emphasize others.

How many rejections have you received in the course of your writing career? How did you deal with being rejected?

To answer your question, dozens of publishers rejected my first manuscript, which I wrote during my years as a student at Oxford! No kidding. And it hurt: There is no such thing as a warm and fuzzy rejection letter. The book never got published, but the process taught me a great deal about the craft of writing a novel. Even more important, it made me realize my own passion for writing. So the point is: Don't ever give up. If you have the passion to create, you must follow it! Persevere!

What's your approach to finishing a book?

The key, I have found, is to find whatever ways you can to get to the end. Complete the thing, even if you're feeling discouraged about it. Then you have something whole to work with, to rewrite or reorder and make into a story that makes you feel proud. For example, sometimes it helps to start the tale, then skip right to the ending while it's fresh, and then fill in the middle. Or you could do as I do, which is to continually rewrite—front to back, front to back, as if you are polishing a sphere. In your revisions, you can always add new themes or characters that add power

Q&A

and originality to your tale. By the time you are done, your sphere will glow with its own unique light!

What's the most important thing you've learned as a writer?

Writing allows me to experience anything I want. It is a great way to live as fully and sensuously as possible—to drink in the richness and diversity, the mystery and terror, the surprise and beauty, of life. It is also a great way to experience many lives at once: As a writer I can find the voice of a twelve-year-old girl, an ancient stone, or a young wizard. Through my characters, I can experience life in the most wondrous ways. If I'm lucky enough to find a character that has lots of richness and depth, such as Merlin, then as the character grows, so do I. And, I hope, so do readers.

What is most rewarding to you about writing?

Writing allows me to explore, wherever and whatever I choose. It has taken me back in time, to a distant galaxy, to the place where the sea begins, to Merlin's magical isle—and many more places as well! Best of all, though, writing is a way to explore the biggest questions of life. Not to find the answers, perhaps, but to do some thoughtful exploring of the questions. The two most rewarding parts of the experience are, first, when a word or character or place or idea comes out just right—and, second, when something I've written truly touches someone else. Some of the letters I've received have been unforgettable enough to keep me up late at night working on the next book.

What's your best advice for people who want to write for teens?

Write an excellent, gripping story that will last for some time—and reach people of all ages. That's what matters most.

Sometimes, when people ask me what age group I write for, I reply: "I write for children of all ages." That is really how I see it. Too often, people who write for young people underestimate

their readers. They oversimplify and write "down" to young people. That is a terrible mistake! Let's give young people more credit for intelligence, curiosity, and serious concern for the future of our planet. So I never write "down": I always treat my readers as intelligent, caring people who are my equals.

In the same vein, we also should not underestimate adults. Many adults still have inside themselves a healthy, vibrant child. Even adults who have lost touch with their inner youth often yearn to rediscover their ability to wonder, to explore, to adventure, to laugh, to feel surprise and awe and mystery. These adults, despite their mature concerns, still possess—or want to possess—the freedom and freshness and openness of youth. That is why I write for adult children, too.

Perhaps this explains why my readers are all ages and descriptions. Yes, I write about heroic young people, such as the young wizard Merlin. But I chose that age for my five books about him because I felt that was the best way to tell that particular story—not because I was aiming my story at a particular audience. The experiences of young Merlin are, I think, a metaphor that could feel true for people of all ages, a metaphor about becoming a wise and caring human being. Similarly, Elli and Tamwyn, who are the heroes in my Avalon trilogy, are both teenagers. But the story is about a subject that appeals to both children and adults: Can humanity learn to live together in peace and harmony with our fellow creatures?

In sum, a writer must be true to his or her own self. That means we need to listen to the story in our hearts, and then write it the very best we can. Then our story, like a small, handcrafted ship, will sail away...and touch shores we can't even imagine.

Q&A

Joan Bauer

www.joanbauer.com

Published books:

Squashed

Thwonk

Sticks

Rules of the Road

Backwater

Hope Was Here

Stand Tall

Best Foot Forward

Peeled

Please say a few words about the YA subgenre in which you write.

I write contemporary YA, although my second novel, *Thwonk*, is a fantasy. I think the power of YA is that it meets kids right where they are and deals with issues that touch them now. The challenge of this for me is to write fiction that illustrates a young person's powerful place in a world filled with vast unfairness and brokenness. I use humor to illuminate as much as I can—and that isn't always easy when I'm talking about alcoholism in a family, dishonor in politics, corporate greed, or misrepresentation in the media. Those are *big* issues and to bring a teen character into them while keeping his or her teen-ness intact is hard. Often in the beginning of a story, I'll start writing the main character in a voice that sounds like me. They can't sound like me; I'm 56 years old. So taking big issues and

AUTHOR Q & A

cutting them down to size and bringing the character into the milieu takes work. I do find it personally exciting, though, when I get that teenage voice right, because to look at big issues as a teen is encouraging, fascinating, and hopeful to me.

How many rejections have you received in the course of your writing career? How did you deal with being rejected?

Early on when I was trying to break in as a screenwriter, I had lots of rejections. I remember one guy left a message on my answering machine saying, "Got your script. Not my cup of tea." Click. Dismissive rejections like that have staying power because after a while they begin to wear you down. I wish I could tell you that I don't take those things personally, but I do. Still, I've also learned that it's important to try to understand what someone might not like about my work, see if they are right, and try to improve. You can't please everyone—if you do, you're probably writing pablum. You also have to know when it's time to defend your work because there is a great deal of bad advice out there, so you can't be the kind of writer who bends to every suggestion and loses the vision of what you were trying to create. As a YA author, my first novel, *Squashed*, won the Delacorte Prize, so I've not had novels rejected. I do have a half finished novel in my drawer that still calls to me late at night. I put it away two years ago because I couldn't finish it. I've learned that all the writing I do—the books that win awards and the ones that don't—are all equally necessary. Each story seems to have a seed of the next book in it somehow. I try to remember that. I try to write the idea that just won't let me go. The one thing you can't let rejection do is stop you from writing. Just start the next story—start it. Starting has great power.

What's your approach to finishing a book?

In later drafts I get an exhilaration at the end, kind of like climbing a mountain and getting close to the summit. Sometimes, though, I'm pretty sick of what I've been working on, and in the later stages, I just push through. I work very long hours at the

end—ten to twelve hours a day. But, you know, giving birth isn't easy!

What's the most important thing you've learned as a writer?

I've learned to not be afraid of the things that have hurt me. I've learned to use those issues in my writing from the point of view of an overcomer.

What is most rewarding to you about writing?

Two things—when I know that my work has made a difference in someone's life; and I just love the part of the creative process when my characters begin to tell me what to do.

What's your best advice for people who want to write for teens?

Respect them. Appeal to their higher natures. Give them hope.

Q&A

Hilari Bell

Published books:

Songs of Power

Navohar (a book for adults)

A Matter of Profit

The Goblin Wood

The Wizard Test

The Prophecy

Fall of a Kingdom (Farsala trilogy 1)

Rise of a Hero (Farsala trilogy 2)

Forging the Sword (Farsala trilogy 3)

Shield of Stars (Shield, Sword & Crown, book 1)

The Last Knight (Knight and Rogue Books, 1)

Please say a few words about the YA subgenre in which you write.

I write YA SF and fantasy. An interviewer once asked me why writing/reading SF and fantasy were important, and I shocked her by replying that writing/reading fiction isn't important. Curing cancer is important. Ending world hunger is important. Heck, putting good brakes on a car is important. Writing fiction? Now don't get me wrong, there's nothing in my life I enjoy more than reading a good book, and I love being a writer almost as much as I love to read. Nothing serious, either! I want an exciting story with some humor, a bit of drama, good characters—and I want my happy ending too! None of this gloomy stuff.

All that said (Off topic? Who, me?) SF really is the literature of ideas—you can explore more interesting concepts in an SF setting than in any other genre. And for character development and excitement, I don't think there's anything that beats fantasy. But important? I'm an entertainer, and I adore it—but I also like to keep it in perspective.

How many rejections have you received in the course of your writing career? How did you deal with being rejected?

I've never actually counted my rejections, but since I wrote for 17 years before I finally had a novel accepted there are lots of them! In fact, I keep hoping that someday I'll get into one of those contests they sometimes hold at writers' conferences for the largest number of rejections judged by weight. I might not win, but I bet I'd make the top ten.

How did I deal with it? Argh! To tell the truth, I think that by the time I should have quit—would have if I'd had any sense—I'd put in so much time and effort that quitting would have been an unhappy ending. I don't read tragedy—I certainly didn't want to live one! So I just kept slogging onward till I finally sold. I should add that, looking back over my early novels, there's a reason why they didn't sell! You have to be good enough. And even when you're good enough there's an appalling amount of luck involved in the process. Getting published is not an easy thing to do, and the best advice I can offer you is to go to writers' conferences as well as SF conventions. I'll also add the most true comment on the topic I've ever encountered: (I heard it from a speaker at a writers' conference, by the way.) "The ones who have been published are the ones who didn't quit."

What's your approach to finishing a book?

My approach to finishing a first draft is to break it down into daily tasks (for me, that's a minimum of eight pages per day, five days a week) and I try not to look ahead at the looming mass of

work. If I've done my daily pages, which I tackle first thing in the morning, then that's all I have to do today, and I'll worry about tomorrow when it comes. I am, however, strict about doing this five days a week, week in week out, till the book is done. If I'm consistent, it adds up to a finished draft pretty quickly.

What's the most important thing you've learned as a writer?

The most important thing I've learned as a writer is probably how to write. There's an incredible amount of craft involved in writing, and looking back at my earlier manuscripts I realize how far I've come. I should probably confess that about half my published novels are "trunk books" that racked up scores of rejections when I first wrote them. But I still liked the stories, and when I hauled them out and rewrote them copiously (or once took the story and wrote it all over from scratch, which in many ways was easier than rewriting) they worked just fine. It wasn't bad stories that kept my books from selling, it was bad writing. And I hope my writing continues to improve for years to come—I never want to stop improving my craft. Never.

What is most rewarding to you about writing?

The most rewarding thing about writing... People always say, "Isn't it exciting to see your name on a book cover?" And I have to admit, it's pretty cool. But the rewarding part isn't looking at your name on the cover, it's when you open the book and there on the pages are your characters, and your dialogue, and your story coming alive. Your story in a book is what's cool—the name on the cover doesn't begin to compare.

What's your best advice for people who want to write for teens?

The best advice I can give anyone writing for teens is to write for yourself first. If you write a story "for teens" you'll probably end up talking from your maturity to their inexperience. A kid will pick up on that and reject it in a heartbeat—and small blame to them! But if you write a story that happens to have teenage

characters—but is mostly just a story that you love, that you want to tell, and that you'd like to read yourself because it's the kind of book you find wonderful—that will work for any reader, of any age. Or at least, any reader who shares your literary tastes, which is the best any writer can expect.

Dia Calhoun

www.diacalhoun.com

Published books:

The Return of Light: A Christmas Tale
Avielle of Rhia
The Phoenix Dance
White Midnight
Aria of the Sea
Firegold

AUTHOR Q&A

Please say a few words about the YA subgenre in which you write.

All of my books are fantasy novels. I love writing about other worlds because it truly lets my imagination take flight. Also, fantasy writers mine the subconscious, burrowing deep into vast underground caverns for their material, and I find that journey fascinating. I love the way metaphors and symbols become so very important in fantasy. In my books, magic often becomes part of the voice of the characters; in other words, there is a relationship between magic and the hero's truest self.

How many rejections have you received in the course of your writing career? How did you deal with being rejected?

It took me five years to sell my first novel, *Firegold*. It was rejected by six publishers. Even after having six published books, I still don't have everything I submit accepted. I deal with rejection by mourning for awhile and eating a king's ransom in chocolate. But I always have

some project going, so I find it easy to distract myself from the rejection, and get on with new work. My agent keeps sending work out.

What's your approach to finishing a book?

I don't have an approach! That's the problem. I worry and worry that I could make the book better. "Just one more revision," I think, and proceed to move a few "the's" around the page. Letting go and sending a book out is like leaving your baby naked on a doorstep and hoping someone kind will find it and love it and tenderly wrap it in swaddling clothes. So it's easier to do just one more revision.

What's the most important thing you've learned as a writer?

I must write about what I feel passionate about, whether it is marketable or not. Writing comes first and publishing comes second. I've learned that if I worry while I'm writing whether something is going to sell or get an award, that completely ruins the creative process for me. My best work comes when I dig deep and don't worry about outcomes.

What is most rewarding to you about writing?

I love the feeling of being a sculptor as I write, chipping away at material bit by bit until the shape of the story emerges. The "ah-ha!" moments when ideas connect with a crackle of excitement and electricity are joyous. And seeing a kid reading one of my books is rewarding, too. Also rewarding is giving back to the reading community, which is why I co-founded readergirlz, an online book community promoting teen literacy, with three other YA authors: Janet Lee Carey, Lorie Ann Grover, and Justina Chen Headley.

What's your best advice for people who want to write for teens?

Read as much YA literature as you can. Find out what teens are concerned about in their daily lives. And remember what

 your life was like when you were a teen. Write every day and don't give up hope. It took me five years to write my first novel, *Firegold*, and five more to sell it. Then two more before it was made into a book. That's TWELVE years. If something is rejected, revise it, or write something new. Don't ever stop writing.

Q&A

Chris Crutcher

www.chriscrutcher.com

Published books:

Running Loose

Stotan!

The Crazy Horse Electric Game

Chinese Handcuffs

Athletic Shorts

The Deep End

Staying Fat for Sarah Byrnes

Ironman

Whale Talk

King of the Mild Frontier

The Sledding Hill

Deadline

Please say a few words about the YA subgenre in which you write.

I write realistic fiction, mostly about teenagers. The challenges are exactly the same as writing realistic fiction about people of any age. I don't have to make the reader believe what I write happened, but I have to make them believe it could have. If I cared about being censored, a special problem would be writing about issues or in a language that doesn't offend people, but I don't, so it doesn't. The biggest challenge in writing realistic fiction is making it real.

**Q&A**

How many rejections have you received in the course of your writing career? How did you deal with being rejected?

If I remember correctly I got rejected by *Reader's Digest* one time and then once with an earlier version of *Running Loose* before I got serious. I was very lucky to find an agent with the next version and she had one or two rejections before she sold it, and was conscious enough of my delicate sensibilities not to tell me about either of them until after she'd made a deal. I was very lucky getting my material into the hands of the right people.

What's your approach to finishing a book?

Hurry. By the time I'm close to finishing it, I just want to get it done. I write very fast and then go back and slow down and add whatever else I need.

What's the most important thing you've learned as a writer?

I wouldn't begin to know how to answer that. The most important things I've learned as a human came with what I do, not what I write about. Writing is just getting down my version of what I see.

What is most rewarding to you about writing?

Truthfully, probably the advances and the royalty checks. It's a tremendously freeing thing to be able to make a living at something I love. But just behind that, it's the responses from readers and the idea that I may have added some small piece to the huge volume of American literature.

What's your best advice for people who want to write for teens?

Know your subject. Respect your subject. Don't preach to them. Tell the truth as you know it and let it fall where it falls.

Mary Peace Finley

www.marypeacefinley.com

Published books:

Soaring Eagle

White Grizzly

Meadow Lark

Little Fox's Secret–The Mystery of Bent's Fort

Tiger Tales

Fernitickles

The Matchbox

Fireflies

Please say a few words about writing for tweens.

At the times in history when the characters in my novels lived, there were no "tweens" or "teens." People were children for a short time, then became adults. My historical novels are, however, for tweens and young adults because of the age of the characters. Regardless of the time in which a story is set or whether the language spoken is antiquated, modern, or futuristic, at the most universal level the characters share common aspirations, dreams, problems, and challenges. Being true to the depth of any character is the key to touching the hearts of our readers. Employing the techniques of the craft of writing—plotting, point of view, description, dialogue—captures our young readers' minds. For young readers, we as authors have the unique opportunity to write about "firsts"—first love, first loss, first death, first questioning of "what is," first comprehension, first exploration into the unknown or forbidden. Once "firsts" have happened, they can never be "firsts" again.

Our coming of age stories have the potential to expand readers' lives and perspectives during what may be the most deeply felt stage of their lives. It's gratifying to hear a reader respond, "Until I read your book, I thought I was the only one who felt that way."

How many rejections have you received in the course of your writing career? How did you deal with being rejected?

Higher mathematics has never been my forte. How many rejections? I don't think I can count that high!

During my first ten years of writing and submitting, I got nothing but rejections for the simple reason that my work wasn't good enough yet. The best thing about the long apprenticeship is that with practice, my writing improved.

It's been a long time now since I've received a rejection, but it could happen again tomorrow. If it does, I'll send my novel out again, hoping for a perfect match.

What's your approach to finishing a book?

For me the end is in the beginning; the beginning is in the end. In plotting out a novel, I know (more or less) what will happen, what conflicts are to be faced on both tangible and intangible levels, and how the story question is resolved.

Nothing ever goes as planned, though. The story grows, changes and evolves along the way.

Instead of one approach to finishing a book, I probably have as many approaches as stories. My mentor, Jane Fitz-Randolph, taught that every story has an inevitable ending and that the author must write toward that inevitable ending. In my latest novel, however, I kept two possible endings in mind all the way through, then struggled with several endings. The struggle for the right ending helped define at greater depth why I'd committed to write the story in the first place. Our stories often say more than we know.

There are as many ways to approach a novel (or finish a novel) as there are writers, and the only right way is your way—what works for you. Some of us begin with a "narrative push," not

knowing where that spark of inspiration will lead; some watch the story progress as if from its own impetus; some plot out the whole story before beginning to write. I suspect that for many of us, it's a mix of all of these.

What's the most important thing you've learned as a writer?

I've learned many "most important things"! On the level of craft—plotting and writing—I've learned to move from one significant action to another significant action and leave out all the rest. On the conceptual level, I've learned to persevere with the original inspiration and yet get out of my head and reconnect with my muse along the way—pose a question about what will happen next, take a nap, sleep on it, wait, listen.

What is most rewarding to you about writing?

I love that first moment of inspiration when a story—sometimes a whole novel—seizes me with so much passion that I can't let it go (or it won't let me go).

What's your best advice for people who want to write for tweens?

Practice. Listen for inspiration. Practice. Learn the craft. Practice. Learning to write well takes as much practice as learning to play the flute. You wouldn't want your first flute lesson to be on stage in front of a huge audience. Your first novel may be a rehearsal. Write it anyway. Learn from it. Writing short stories hones the same skills as writing a novel and takes less time. Listen to the voices and struggles of young people or listen to the tween who lives within you.

Seek opportunities to improve your writing: critique groups, "how to" books, classes, workshops, conferences. Then as your writing skills become old hat, seek opportunities to deepen and expand sources of inspiration, information, and experience for your work (e.g., a rafting trip or a screenwriting class).

Nancy Garden

www.nancygarden.com

Some of her published books (complete list on website):

Annie on My Mind

Hear Us Out: Lesbian and Gay Stories of Struggle, Progress, and Hope, 1950 to the Present

Dove & Sword: A Novel of Joan of Arc

Good Moon Rising

Prisoner of Vampires

Peace, O River

Please say a few words about the YA subgenre in which you write.

I've written in a number of subgenres: fantasy, contemporary, horror, gay and lesbian, mystery, history. Each one presents its own challenges, although all require the same basic ingredients: believable, consistent characters; a credible setting; logical plot development; overall honesty.

Fantasy and horror need world-creating to a greater or lesser extent depending on the specific story, and that can be very challenging; I especially admire authors who've created complex worlds unlike our own—Tolkien, of course, especially, and Pullman. My books in those genres are far simpler, and much more closely allied to our own world.

The challenge in mystery is to weave enough red herrings into the plot to mislead the reader and at the same time plant real clues that, at the end, make the reader say "Oh, of course!"—or at least not shout, "But that's not fair—nothing was *said* about that!"

In historical fiction, the challenge is to reflect the period so accurately that the reader is removed from the present era—and never to jolt the reader by, for example, suddenly introducing a contemporary object—say, a fork that hasn't yet been invented—or using an expression (like "Okay!") that no one in that era would have said.

The current challenge in gay and lesbian (GL) fiction is to move with the times and write stories in which GL characters are no longer defeated victims—okay, that's a political challenge perhaps more than a literary one. Another challenge in both GL books and in serious contemporary fiction as a whole is not letting "message" overwhelm story. In any contemporary fiction for teens, too, the challenge is to keep up with the times or find believable ways to avoid them. I'm talking about the trappings of "teendom"—things like cell phones and clothes and music and dating behavior and slang (keeping in mind that the details of all of these, especially slang, change faster than most books' production schedules move forward).

How many rejections have you received in the course of your writing career? How did you deal with being rejected?

I've received many, but I've never kept count so I can't answer that question. At first, I was very upset at rejections, especially those that didn't offer helpful suggestions—I wanted to throw my typewriter (yes: typewriter, back then!) across the room or cry. But now I'm much calmer!

What's your approach to finishing a book?

I guess the best way to answer that is to sketch how I usually go about writing a book. Every book is different, of course, but each time when I start a new one, I wonder if I really know how. Then I work at ignoring that thought! I usually don't start a book until it's been gestating in my mind for a long time—frequently years—so I usually have a pretty good idea of what it's about, who's in it, and how it ends. I write a rough (very

rough!) draft all the way through quickly, often outlining along the way and changing the outline as I go. I also write brief character autobiographies (I pretend to *be* the characters) at some early point as well, but usually not until I've drafted a few chapters or sections and seen a bit of how the characters behave.

I never stop work for the day until I know what I'm going to start with the next day—that's one thing that definitely keeps me going forward. And I rarely stop to perfect sentences, paragraphs, etc., until I'm revising. After the first or second revisions, I usually put the book away for a while—months or more—so that when I go back to it, I'll be able to see its flaws more clearly. At that point, I go on revising until, as a writer friend of mine once said, I can't see anything more to do. Then I give the manuscript to my partner, who's my first reader—and that usually leads to more revising, till it finally seems ready to send to my agent.

What's the most important thing you've learned as a writer?

I've learned many important things, but I guess the most important is that it's vital to try to keep on writing no matter what—even when one doesn't feel like it. And it's also important to remember that a writer's career—mine, anyway—contains both ups and downs, and that it's important to plow through the downs, keep writing, and have faith that the ups will return.

What is most rewarding to you about writing?

Getting a letter from a reader that indicates a book of mine has spoken to that reader, touched her or him deeply, and helped in some way.

What's your best advice for people who want to write for teens?

Read, read, read—and read some more. And write, write, write—and write some more!

Emmanuel Guibert

Emmanuel Guibert is a French author/illustrator of graphic novels.

Published books in the United States:

Sardine in Outer Space (many volumes)
The Professor's Daughter (co-authored with Joann Sfar)
Alan's War

Many other books have been published in France and other countries.

Please say a few words about writing graphic novels.

I'm both a writer and an illustrator. I write for myself, I write for others and others write for me. Each of these positions is interesting, and quite different from the others. The first one is like jogging by oneself in an unknown landscape. The second is like jogging side by side with a friend in an unknown landscape, pretending you're the one who knows the way. The third is like jogging side by side with a friend in an unknown landscape, confident that your friend knows the way, but memorizing it very carefully because you know that, on the way back, it will be your turn to lead.

Anyway, in the three situations, you're always running.

How many rejections have you received in the course of your writing career? How did you deal with being rejected?

Any time I'm rejected, Mom is there to heal the pain.

What's your approach to finishing a book?

A book is finished long before being finished. It's when you start thinking about the next one, and preparing it. My oven is full of different pies, cooking at different speeds.

What's the most important thing you've learned as a writer?

To think about adults when I write for children, and think about children when I write for adults.

What is most rewarding to you about writing?

A nine-year-old reader, whom I met at an exhibition, once told me, "Your stories are good, because first I read them, and then they happen to me." I considered that quite rewarding.

Q&A

Patrick Jones

www.connectingya.com

Myspace: www.myspace.com/connectingya

Published books:

Things Change

Nailed

Chasing Tail Lights

Cheated

Stolen Car

Please say a few words about the YA subgenre in which you write.

I write a very narrow slice of the market: realistic fiction for older teens. It is narrow because many older teens (10th grade and up) no longer read YA fiction, and narrower yet, because to write for this age group, it means raw honesty. Raw in terms of language, themes, and subjects. This further narrows the market since for many teens the gatekeepers for books are teachers who often shy away from using my novels. The primary challenge—other than writing for the narrow market—is working with editors on how honest to make the work: how much graphic sexual content, substance use, and profanity.

How many rejections have you received in the course of your writing career? How did you deal with being rejected?

My first novel, *Things Change*, was rejected three times. I avoided further rejection by not submitting it again for ten years. My path to publication is a little different than most. Through my career working in a library I'd made contacts in the book industry and

thus was able to hand my manuscript to an editor without going through an agent. An editor rejected it the first time, and then the rewrite, until I got it "right" on the third try. My rejection is more post publication, which is dealing with my books being rejected by committees like Best Books for Young Adults or Minnesota Book Awards. I don't deal with it well, to be honest. I normally go back and reread some of the e-mails or myspace messages from teens who tell me how much they enjoyed one of my books.

What's your approach to finishing a book?

A very important step for me is getting teens to read my work before I submit it to my publisher. I've worked with one particular high school nearby that gathers kids who want the experience of reading and commenting on a manuscript together. They read it, and then I go discuss it with them. I also make that offer to teens who e-mail me or that I meet doing school visits. I don't feel a book is "finished" anymore until I know that teens have given me the green light.

What's the most important thing you've learned as a writer?

As my editor would tell you, it is not how to punctuate! The real lesson is patience: this work takes time. That's not really a virtue I possess, and I also write my first drafts in huge writing jags over a couple of months. The patience comes with the rewriting, revising, and production from that "high" of getting it on paper for the first time until it comes out almost 16 months later.

What is most rewarding to you about writing?

Feedback from readers during school visits, on myspace, by e-mail, or old-school letter in the mail. Knowing that something you wrote impacted a young person's life, maybe changed it for the better—that's pretty important stuff. Also, eating french fries during school visits.

What's your best advice for people who want to write for teens?

This work is about empathy. If you can't bring yourself to empathize with the journey that every teenager is taking, then writing successfully for this market will be very difficult. I'd also suggest reading a couple of the touchstone books in the field: *The Outsiders, Speak, Rats Saw God,* and a few others so you can discover the one thing that seems to join together the great works isn't theme or story, but voice.

Q&A

Elise Leonard
www.eliseleonard.com

Published books:

Al's World books:

    Monday Morning Blitz

    Killer Lunch Lady

    Scared Stiff

    Monkey Business

Please say a few words about writing for tweens.

    I love writing for tweens! Particularly boys. After teaching for many years, I seem to have picked up their way of thinking and sense of humor. This is, at times, quite unfortunate for me—being almost half a century old—and is even less fortunate for my almost-always mortified sons. For example, at a recent highly dignified black-tie (adult only) event linking authors with literary patrons, while passing through the buffet line, at the cheese table displaying huge wheels of assorted cheeses, after noticing that there was no knife, I turned to those around me and asked if anyone had a knife so I could cut the cheese. Then, in a most undignified manner, I cracked up hysterically. Needless to say, I was the only one laughing, after which I felt the need to mumble, "Get it? Cut the cheese?" with no response whatsoever from the surrounding adults, which made me crack up again, even more hysterically. (And in case you're wondering, I had not passed the alcoholic beverage table before hitting the cheese table. I was clearheaded and perfectly sober. My reaction was all me—au naturel.)

How many rejections have you received in the course of your writing career? How did you deal with being rejected?

Ah. Rejections. Rejections are part of a writer's life just as corrections are part of a student's life. And please note—rejections are a large part of a writer's life. Sometimes, if you're lucky, you can learn from the rejection, particularly if you respect the person who is making the comments or voicing their concerns. Other times, there is nothing to learn.

It's important to understand that every person likes something different (whether it's music, art, movies or books) so it can be wise to keep that in mind after receiving a rejection. But still, there are those die hard "opinionists" (as my husband likes to call them) who are not out to improve your work or story but may just enjoy being able to say no.

I haven't always agreed with all the comments I've received, but the ones from people I respect, I must admit, have truly been constructive criticism. How I deal with being rejected stems largely from how I feel about the person doing the rejecting. But I must admit that at first, years ago, I did go through what you will probably go through in the beginning of your writing career: a nice private hissy fit, followed by anger, embarrassment, a feeling of loss, then a long period of hurt followed by numbness, then, with time, healing and, finally, renewed strength and vigor. Just in time to start that whole process all over again.

But, for me, after a while of doing that, it just got too exhausting. My response was much too emotionally and physically draining! So I toned it down a peg or two (or five thousand!) for my own sanity (and that of my poor husband and my almost-always mortified sons). Now I'm down to rolling my eyes and saying, "Oh, well. Their loss! And I wouldn't want to work with that person anyhow!" Then I might stick out my tongue or blow a raspberry, depending on my mood at the time (if the person was even worth the extra effort).

What's your approach to finishing a book?

My approach to finishing a book is quite simple. I start it. I keep working on it. I work on it some more. Until I finish it. Then I read it again. Fix it. Fix it again. Fix it some more. Until I'm done fixing it. Then I read it again. Then, if it's okay, I stop. If not, I fix it again, and then I stop.

What's the most important thing you've learned as a writer?

The most important thing I've learned as a writer is...don't quit your day job. Or, if you do quit your day job, have a really nice husband, partner or parent who will support you totally—financially, emotionally, nutritionally, and in any and all other ways possible or imaginable! So, in other words, don't do it for the money or the sole purpose of getting published. Write because you love doing it and can't stop doing it. Write because there is nothing else you'd rather do! Write because it brings you joy whether someone else reads a word of it or not. That's why I do it.

What is most rewarding to you about writing?

The most rewarding thing about writing for me is the response from the kids who like my books. For me, there is no other reward.

What's your best advice for people who want to write for tweens?

My best advice for people who want to write for tweens is to know tweens!

David Lubar

www.davidlubar.com

Some of his published books (more listed on website):

True Talents

Hidden Talents

Sleeping Freshmen Never Lie

Dunk

Flip

Wizards of the Game

Invasion of the Road Weenies

The Curse of the Campfire Weenies

In the Land of the Lawn Weenies

Punished!

Dog Days

Please say a few words about the YA subgenre in which you write.

My work is scattered across a variety of subgenres, including fantasy, science fiction, and horror. I guess the thing I'm best known for is humor. There are both external and internal challenges for writing humor. Externally, funny books don't get as much respect as serious books. (Balancing that, they can be pretty popular with readers and with the teachers and librarians who try to generate enthusiasm for books.) Internally, the greatest difficulty in writing humor for teens is making sure that the material is relevant to their interests, and that any references would be within their universe. You won't get many laughs if you make references to Eisenhower or slide rules. But you also can't fall into the trap of using contemporary

 references that might become meaningless in a couple of years. (Translation: no Sanjaya jokes.)

How many rejections have you received in the course of your writing career? How did you deal with being rejected?

I gathered more than 100 rejections before making any sort of sale. I tried to motivate myself by noting the slow improvement from form slips to jotted notes to actual letters where editors seemed sincere in their dismay about not being able to purchase my work. Even now, with 17 published books and tons of published short stories, I still don't like rejection.

What's your approach to finishing a book?

I keep banging at it until one of us dies. So far, when the dust cleared, I've been the one still standing. I try to keep up a good pace each day. If I get bogged down, I'll take a breath and work up an outline. (I generally dive in without one.) If I get really stuck, I'll write a rambling dialogue with myself , discussing the problem. I keep talking on paper until an answer appears.

What's the most important thing you've learned as a writer?

You can always improve. There's no end to learning the craft.

What is most rewarding to you about writing?

Creating something from nothing. When a character speaks a great line, or a plot takes an unexpected turn, I feel grateful to my subconscious, or whatever mechanism is responsible for making things happen.

What's your best advice for people who want to write for teens?

Don't write down. It is crucial to respect the reader. Don't avoid complexity or depth. Don't treat a teen like a child. Write an amazing story, sharing something you've gained or learned in life. Oh—and don't kill the main character's best friend just because it's an easy way to create drama.

Q&A

Carolyn Meyer

www.readcarolyn.com

Some of her published books (more listed on website):

Young Royals series:

> *Mary, Bloody Mary*
>
> *Beware, Princess Elizabeth*
>
> *Doomed Queen Anne*
>
> *Patience, Princess Catherine*
>
> *Duchessina: A Novel of Catherine de' Medici*

Scholastic, Royal Diary series:

> *Isabel, Jewel of Castilla*
>
> *Anastasia, Last Grand Duchess*
>
> *Kristina, The Girl King*

Where the Broken Heart Still Beats: the Story of Cynthia Ann Parker

Marie, Dancing

Loving Will Shakespeare

Please say a few words about the YA subgenre in which you write.

I write historical fiction. Kids often ask me, "Is it true?" What they mean, I think, is, "Are your facts right?" And the answer is yes—insofar as I can find out the historical facts, and I spend a huge amount of time on research, gathering as many facts as I can. When the facts are not in agreement—and in history, they often are not—then I choose the facts that make the best narrative. I don't rewrite history, but once the known facts are in place, I invent like mad. One big challenge is finding the right voice for the narrator:

AUTHOR Q&A

how do you sound like Shakespeare without writing Shakespearean English? Another challenge is avoiding the Dread Anachronism, especially in language. I work hard at that, but I've been nailed a few times.

How many rejections have you received in the course of your writing career? How did you deal with being rejected?

When I first started to write 45 years ago, I sent all my marvelous short stories to *The New Yorker* which promptly rejected them all. But when I found my niche, writing for kids (I started in how-to, progressed to more complicated nonfiction, then moved into fiction, and finally, about 15 years ago, into historical fiction), rejection was no longer the norm. I've written more than 50 books; only one has been rejected. The question I think you should be asking is, "How do you deal with criticism?" Because I get a TON of that. I've been fortunate to have excellent editors who hold the bar very high indeed, and I often have to go through three complete rewrites of my "perfect" manuscript before it meets their standards.

What's your approach to finishing a book?

I find that discipline compensates for brilliance and talent. I go for a 2-1/2 mile walk every morning, eat my oatmeal, and sit down at my desk by 9 a.m. I quit at 5. I put in time on weekends. I drink a lot of tea.

What's the most important thing you've learned as a writer?

Mostly I've learned exactly who I am. I've been working full time at writing for 45 years, and I've gotten pretty good at it. There were times when I got discouraged (I wasn't making any money to speak of), but I've never wanted to do anything else.

What is most rewarding to you about writing?

Knowing that I reach kids, touch their lives, and maybe even expand their horizons—I know it happens, because I get a lot of e-mail from readers.

What's your best advice for people who want to write for teens?

Stomp on anybody who asks you at a party, "But when are you going to start writing for adults?" Writing for teens is the real deal. Satisfaction guaranteed!

Q&A

Claudia Mills
www.claudiamillsauthor.com

Some of her published books (more listed on website):

The Totally Made-Up Civil War Diary of Amanda MacLeish
Trading Places
Makeovers by Marcia
Alex Ryan, Stop That!
Dinah Forever
Losers, Inc.
Standing Up to Mr. O
You're a Brave Man, Julius Zimmerman

Please say a few words about writing for tweens.

When you write for tweens you need to have the paradoxical ability both to think that the crises your fictional adolescents are facing are indeed crises and the most important thing going on anywhere in the world—in the universe!—and at the same time to think that ultimately these events are not catastrophic life upheavals, but routine parts of growing up faced in some way by everyone, everywhere. On the one hand, you need to take seriously how tweens understand their own experiences and honor the life and death urgency they impart to them, and on the other hand, to deflate this seriousness with some adult perspective, and even, and especially, with humor. I often say that I write survival narratives, but what my characters are surviving is not being stranded alone in the wilderness in a winter storm: they are surviving the much more threatening and painful experience of the seventh grade dance.

How many rejections have you received in the course of your writing career? How did you deal with being rejected?

I have probably received many fewer rejections than the typical author, but I'm probably one of the only authors who has ever been forced to reject my own manuscript! Let me explain.

I got my start as a children's author when I worked for Four Winds Press/Scholastic in the late 1970s. I was a secretary to three editors there, and my duties included reading manuscripts from the slush pile, writing manuscript reports, typing editorial correspondence (on an IBM Selectric typewriter), answering the phone, and sending out for iced tea or other snacks when one of those glorious beings—a real live author—came in for an editorial conference.

I had a long commute back and forth to Manhattan from my home in Princeton, NJ, and on the bus I busily scribbled away on manuscripts of my own, which I started submitting to various houses, to uniform rejection. My rejections were all standard form letters, so I was getting no helpful feedback at all on how to improve in my craft. Then I hit upon the brilliant idea of submitting one of my manuscripts to Four Winds Press/Scholastic, my own house, under a pseudonym, so my three editor bosses wouldn't know it was me. That way I could be a fly on the wall, observing the process with my own inquisitive eyes. My manuscript arrived in the mail; Barbara Lalicki read and rejected it—and I, as her secretary, had to type my own rejection letter. That was a very melancholy task indeed!

Undaunted, I sent in a second story and typed a second rejection letter to myself. But the third time, Barbara thought the story had more promise, and she asked me to read it and give her my written critique. To my great surprise, upon reading it, this time with an editorial rather than authorial eye, I saw flaws in my work I had never seen before, and I ended up writing Barbara an honest and balanced assessment of the piece: its strengths, its weaknesses, and how it could be strengthened through revision. Barbara wrote a letter to the author (me),

which her secretary (me) typed, and the letter said, "I am sending you a copy of my reader's report on your manuscript. If you are willing to revise the manuscript according to the suggestions in the report, I would like to see it again and consider it for publication." I did exactly that, and Four Winds Press ended up publishing the book under the title *At the Back of the Woods*. Luckily for me, Barbara had a good sense of humor. I see her at conferences sometimes, and she is still chuckling about it, all these years later.

After that, I have to say, I received very few rejections. Beverly Reingold, another of my three Four Winds Press supervisors, became my editor, and she and I have been together now for over 25 years and over 40 books. Because I know that she believes in me, and in my books, and in my ability to revise, if she rejects one of my books (which she sometimes does), I would never consider submitting it elsewhere. I either try to revise it to her specifications, or let it go and write something else instead.

What's your approach to finishing a book?

I don't think I could write books, and certainly I couldn't finish a book, without having a critique group to support me in my writing and to tell me whether or not I am on the right track. I used to live in Maryland where I was a member of a critique group called The Soup Group. We met every other Tuesday for critique and lunch – and yes, for lunch we had soup. Now I live in Colorado where I have been a member of the same wonderful group for fifteen years. Here we meet every other Monday evening.

My critique group helps me finish a book because I don't want to come to a meeting empty-handed: many of my chapters have been written on the day of critique group and wouldn't have been written without that deadline. And they help me finish a book because they point out, sometimes with painful precision, exactly where they think I am going right with my story, and where I am going wrong. I don't have to paralyze myself with endless second-guessing. If my group laughs, I know they

think my chapter is funny, and that means it *is* funny. Likewise, if they think a scene is confusing, or the character of the father is too unlikable, or a subplot is weak, then I know exactly what I need to do.

What's the most important thing you've learned as a writer?

The most important thing I've learned as a writer is to trust the process. Even after writing and publishing over 40 books, I still feel utterly lost as I begin a new book. "How *do* you write a book?" I think. How does anyone sit down and look at that blank page and begin writing words on it? What if the words aren't any good? Then what do I do? Even after all these books, published with the same editor whom I adore and trust completely, every time she sends me her critique of one of my books, I'm devastated. I can't see any way of fixing the book; I feel that I need to tear it up into little pieces and throw it away and start on something completely different, or better yet, *not* start on another book at all, but abandon writing for a whole other career.

What I've learned is that if I do what I'm supposed to do, it will all turn out to be all right. That is, if I sit down every day and write a page or two, it will add up to a few hundred pages at the end of a year. If, consumed with fear and self-loathing, I make myself show these terrible, embarrassing pages to my critique group, they will help me see that my pages are not so terrible and embarrassing after all, and they will help me to make them much less terrible and embarrassing. If I listen to what my editor tells me, after the requisite period of sulking, I will find a way to revise the book to make it a thousand times better than it was before. And then if need be, I can revise it a second time, and a third, or a fourth. The process works! It really does work! Just write, submit your work for critique, listen to the critique, revise in response to the critique, and your book will get better. It really will!

What is most rewarding to you about writing?

For me, the most rewarding thing about writing is the writing itself. I am not one of those writers who doesn't like to write, but likes having written. It's the writing itself I love best. I have all these delightful rituals. I write longhand, on a pad of white narrow ruled paper, with no margins, using my favorite Pilot Razorpoint fine tipped black marker pen, leaning on the same clipboard I've used for the past thirty years—the clip on it broke off long ago, and it has one dented corner from where I threw it at my college boyfriend. I always drink the same beverage while I write: Swiss Miss hot chocolate. I write lying down, on a couch or in my bed. I write only for an hour a day, because I have another full-time job, as a college professor, and I'm also a busy mom. That one hour for me is an hour of bliss, as the words fill the page, and characters say things much cleverer than anything I could have thought up for them to say, and surprise me with the brave and heartbreaking and funny things they do. I just love to write.

What's your best advice for people who want to write for tweens?

To write about tweens, you need to know tweens. There are several ways to do this. For years, I wrote from my own vivid memories of being a tween. I mined those memories for book after book and still feel that I have hardly scratched the surface of all my agonies of fifth grade, sixth grade, seventh grade. I think I could write just about my own fifth grade year for the rest of my life. So, do everything you can to remember your own tween years. Play music of the period (for me, "Cherish" by the Association was the big slow dance song for the junior high dances), look at any scraps of memorabilia you saved (I still have notes furtively exchanged during math class from my seventh grade girlfriends). Face it all honestly. Remember most of all the things you've worked for several decades to forget.

If you have kids of your own, pay attention. After years of writing about girls, I became the mother of two boys, and now I write even more stories about boys than I do about girls. Volunteer to drive the carpool and listen to what the kids say. Help out in the classroom. Sign up to chaperone at the middle school dance. You will find ten stories every single day!

Finally, if you've exhausted your own memories, and you don't have kids or your kids are grown, find other ways to be in the company of tweens. Stop by the middle school and offer your services. Spend an afternoon as a spy in the mall. Every time they open their mouths, a story is there for the taking. Take it.

Q&A

Todd Mitchell

www.toddmitchellbooks.com

Published books:

The Traitor King

Syzygy (Working title. Publication in 2009)

Please say a few words about the YA subgenre in which you write.

I have a hard time describing what genre I write in. My first novel, *The Traitor King,* is considered fantasy aimed at a 4-7th grade audience, although much of the book happens in this world. My second novel is realistic character driven fiction aimed at a high school audience, although fantastic things happen in that book. Basically, I'm interested in intersections —stories where fantasy and reality cross over. The world is full of strange things. What some might consider fantasy often feels more true to me than strictly realistic fiction.

How many rejections have you received in the course of your writing career? How did you deal with being rejected?

I never counted my rejections, but there were many. Suffice it to say, I thought it would only take me a few years to get a book published. Instead, it took me over ten years.

One thing that kept me going was when a friend of mine, who happens to be a completely amazing best-selling author, confessed to me that she wrote seven "practice" novels before getting one accepted. For me, the magic number was four. The good news,

though, is that I got better with every novel, and when I finally wrote one that I knew was ready, it got accepted right away.

What's your approach to finishing a book?

I try to write the first draft fairly quickly (in around four months). I give myself a goal of two to three pages every day and try to keep moving forward without getting too obsessed about rewriting the beginning a hundred times. Even though I usually start off following some sort of outline with the first draft, things always change as I write. So this first draft is how I figure out what my story is about and who my characters are.

Once I've written a first draft, I might put it aside for a few weeks to gain perspective, then I'll come back to it and start rewriting. I tend to spend two to three times as long rewriting my books as I do actually writing the first drafts. This is where I tease the story out, explore my characters, and make things readable. Then I'll share the book with a few critical readers and revise it again. And, of course, when I finally send it off to editors, they'll request more changes.

What's the most important thing you've learned as a writer?

Stick with it. I can't tell you how many times I thought about giving up, but nothing else satisfied me as deeply as writing did. The beauty of writing is that the more you do it, the better you get at it. Being a writer has far more to do with perseverance than talent.

What is most rewarding to you about writing?

For years, I thought the most rewarding thing about writing would be to get letters from people who'd enjoyed my books. Now that that's happened, I can honestly say it's not the most rewarding thing. Don't get me wrong—I love getting letters. But the most rewarding thing is simply getting to write more stories. That's something I wish I'd known before I was published because I think it would have helped me to stop worrying so

much about publishing and instead focus on the writing. I strongly believe that publishing will come when the book is ready, but the act of writing itself is the greatest reward.

What's your best advice for people who want to write for teens?

Read a lot of young adult fiction. Spend time with adolescents. Revive your inner teen. And don't listen to people who suggest that writing for young adults is somehow lesser than "adult literary fiction"—they just haven't discovered how daring, complex, and truly amazing young adult fiction is these days.

Q&A

Lauren Myracle

www.laurenmyracle.com

Published books:

Bliss

Kissing Kate

Eleven

Twelve

Thirteen

TTYL

TTFN

L8R, G8R

Rhymes with Witches

The Fashion Disaster that Changed My Life

How to Be Bad (co-authored with E. Lockhart and Sarah Mlynowski)

Please say a few words about the YA subgenre in which you write.

I write straight up contemporary fiction. Kind of. (Nothing in this field is totally straight up, I guess!) I write about girls and their daily lives and concerns, mainly. Sometimes it's hard, because the grown-up "gatekeepers" (teachers, librarians, parents) have a different take on what's appropriate to write about (and think about) than I do. But being fearless—and at the same time principled, of course, according to your own principles—just comes with the territory.

AUTHOR Q&A

How many rejections have you received in the course of your writing career? How did you deal with being rejected?

Okay, um, ready? One hundred fifty-two rejections. You heard it right, baby. One hundred fifty-two rejections before I got my first novel accepted! At first each rejection devastated me, and I would fling myself on the couch and mope and feel sorry for myself. And then I got tough and realized that I could either quit, and guarantee that I'd never get published, or keep on struggling. I kept on struggling.

What's your approach to finishing a book?

Butt in chair. Just do it.

What's the most important thing you've learned as a writer?

To let my brain be open to possibilities—and to be willing to hurt my characters. Sounds awful, doesn't it? I don't mean I'm going to whack 'em over the head with a plank (though I might). I just mean that I've finally learned that keeping my characters safe doesn't make for a good story. I've got to allow them to be hurt emotionally, so that they can grow.

What is most rewarding to you about writing?

Well, I *do* love the rush of having my brain engaged, once I get past the dragging of feet and doing of laundry that sometimes gets in the way. Other than that, I love having girls *read my stuff* and tell me that it meant something to them.

What's your best advice for people who want to write for teens?

Read books for teens! Seriously. Sounds like a no-brainer, but so many people I've met who say they want to write for teens aren't actually familiar with the (awesome! fabulous! *Not* dumbed-down!) genre.

Q&A

photo © Ian Schneider

Laura Resau

Published books:

What the Moon Saw
Red Glass

Please say a few words about the YA subgenre in which you write.

I write multicultural magical realism. *What the Moon Saw* and *Red Glass* were inspired by the two years I spent in rural Mexico as an English teacher and cultural anthropologist. Both books involve teens who are initially outsiders to the indigenous Mixtec culture, yet develop a strong connection with it. I think that spending time in indigenous communities helped me create authentic and vivid settings, characters, and imagery. In particular, participating in healing practices with curandera friends allowed me to naturally integrate spiritual or "magical" elements into otherwise realistic stories.

During the writing and revising process, I frequently fact-checked details via e-mail with my Mixtec friends, who gave me feedback on everything from slang words to corn cultivation. My Mexican and Guatemalan friends here in the U.S. generously went through every bit of dialogue with a fine-tooth comb, offering their suggestions and thoughts. In gratitude to the countless people who contributed to my books along the way, I'm donating a percentage of my royalties to indigenous rights organizations. Writing these books has truly been a group effort.

AUTHOR · Q & A

How many rejections have you received in the course of your writing career? How did you deal with being rejected?

For my first book, *What the Moon Saw*, I received a total of about twelve rejections from agents and editors. In retrospect, I know that's not too bad, but every rejection caused me plenty of angst. I constantly wondered if the hours I spent writing every day were a giant waste of time. I felt guilty that I didn't have a regular nine-to-five job, pathetic that I was depending on my husband to pay most of our bills, and even more pathetic that I couldn't find time to do my share of the dishes or housecleaning.

As I was battling doubts, one thing that worked well was imagining myself in seventy years, as an old woman looking back on my life. I would ask this old woman what mattered most at this time of my life. Her answer was never doing the dishes or cleaning the toilet. What always mattered most was writing.

What's your approach to finishing a book?

After I have a rough draft (basically an uncensored stream-of-consciousness piece of writing), I ask myself how I can bring the story's themes into greater relief, further explore characters and relationships, develop the story's natural structure, clarify subplots, and draw out emotional layers. Once I've dealt with these broad issues, I break the manuscript down into manageable ten-page chunks and try to revise a chunk per day. I do many revisions, continually tightening, cutting, and adding. My writing group and my mom give me invaluable feedback during this process, until we all feel that the manuscript is polished and ready to submit.

What's the most important thing you've learned as a writer?

My biggest struggle as a writer has been dealing with insecurities and anxieties surrounding writing. The specific nature of the anxiety has changed over the years, depending on my circumstances. What if this manuscript never gets published—have I wasted thousands of hours? What if I can't do the revisions my editor wants? What if I can never create another good book? And on and on.

By now, I understand that I can't escape these insecurities—I can only put them into perspective and choose not to pay too much attention to them. I conceive of them as a pesky, shape-shifting monster that's always trying to undermine my creativity. Now I can recognize the monster in his disguise and say, "Oh, it's you again," then do my best to ignore him, and keep writing.

What is most rewarding to you about writing?

The books that have most deeply affected my worldview have been books that I read when I was young. As a teen, my concept of the universe was still very fluid, and a good book could open new realms of existence to me. I could very easily lose myself in a fantastical world in a book, and I relished how it permeated the rest of my life.

Now, as an author, I feel honored and thrilled to be a creator of these worlds. I love getting letters from readers who feel that my books transported them to a world they didn't want to leave, or that my books have changed the way they see the world and themselves.

What's your best advice for people who want to write for teens?

I think that a powerful novel comes from a very deep, mysterious place. It doesn't result from analyzing market trends or intending to teach a lesson or trying to explicitly address a "teen issue." Good teen books are just as multilayered and resonant and deep as adult books, or even more so. In my experience, writing fiction for any age group is a dance between the dream mind and the rational mind—with the dream mind leading.

My advice is to respect this creative process and feel grateful you're part of it. The ancient poet-philosopher Rumi compared humans to hollow reed flutes—it is only when breath passes through that music is made. When I'm feeling stuck in my writing, I remind myself that I only need to be a hollow reed and let the story come through me.

Q&A

Lynda Sandoval

www.lyndasandoval.com

Published books:

Who's Your Daddy?
Chicks Ahoy
"Party Foul," in *Breaking Up is Hard to Do*

Please say a few words about the YA genre in which you write.

I like to describe what I write as teens "who happen to be" fiction. Can I have my own genre? My books tackle universal, contemporary, realistic teen themes, but my characters often "happen to be" multicultural, or "happen to be" gay or lesbian. Why the "happen to be" designation? Well, because the fact that a character is Latina or Black or mixed-race ethnicity or gay/lesbian isn't what solely defines him or her, nor is it the sole focus of my stories. It's merely one facet of the teen experience he or she faces, one aspect of each book I write.

How did I end up in this non-genre genre? Well, I happen to be both mixed ethnicity (Latina/Scandinavian) and gay, but neither of these fully defined my growing up experience. It shaped it, sure. Like spices in a pot of paella, it gave my own coming-of-age a certain flavor, but for the most part, all the normal teen stuff in my life was...well, utterly, heinously normal! It's hard to describe it any other way. I wanted to write books, as an example, for Latinas who didn't grow up in the widely perceived stereotypical "Latina" situation. We didn't speak Spanish at home because my mom isn't Latina, however I understand a lot of Spanish from having heard my

father speak to my grandparents (when he didn't want me to eavesdrop—they all spoke fluent English, too). I actually speak English and German, and that's because I lived in Germany for four years in my early 20s. My gigantic family includes mixed-race cousins such as Latina/Asian (Korean), Latina/Black, Latina/Caucasian. I have cousins with children fluent in English, Spanish, and Japanese. My world has never been a pure white canvas, and yet we were born and raised in mainstream America. So a rainbow cast of people is just reality to me. It wasn't something I decided to write because it was hot, it's just my world view.

I also wanted to write what my editor calls "fun gay fiction," because, although it's a crucial and defining step, the coming out experience isn't horrific for everyone—it certainly wasn't for me. It is for many, and I want to include that in my work as well. But what about those kids with enlightened and accepting parents, with support, unconditional love? Don't they deserve books they can relate to as well? I thought so, hence my current editorial direction.

I volunteer in a GLBTQ (Gay, Lesbian, Bisexual, Transgender, Queer or Questioning) youth drop-in center, and those kids, whom I adore, are as diverse as any group of teens you might encounter. Trust me. They wouldn't all be interested in the same books. They—all of them—deserve a voice, and I hope to toss in my hat with the other amazing authors writing GLBTQ fiction, in order to do them justice, bring them to the forefront. They're just teens, struggling through the hell that is adolescence (I say that tongue in cheek) in the best way they know how. God bless them.

So that's my story. I write teens "who happen to be" fiction, and I couldn't be happier about it. I don't want to be locked in a box. I want to write fringe work that's also mainstream. Real life. The through-lines in my teen fiction, if I had to narrow them down, would be (1) snappy tone, (2) humor, (3) true teen struggles, and (4) wicked teen empowerment. I connect with

teens so much. I really get them, and my respect for them is boundless. I only hope that comes through in my work.

How many rejections have you received in the course of your writing career? How did you deal with being rejected?

A long time ago, in a land far, far away (okay, Germany when I was in my early 20s), I sat in a laundromat reading from *Writing the Novel: From Plot to Print*, by Lawrence Block. He made rejection truly seem like just a part of the game, another step, and I adopted that attitude immediately. Rejections were a bummer, certainly, mostly for the lost time. But they never felt like crushing blows to me and still don't. They are what they are. I was lucky to receive my first contract only three years after I'd begun writing, so I didn't amass that many rejections, relatively speaking. But, when I used to freelance, I once received a form rejection to a simple request for writers' guidelines! That was fun. I still have it.

What's your approach to finishing a book?

I have to write from the beginning to the end, revising as I go, and only one book at a time. I need to be immersed in that book. I'm not a draft writer per se. I don't write the full book and then go back and revise—way too daunting. I write-revise-write-revise-write-revise all the way until the end. My final read through is usually easy because, after all that, the work is pretty clean. I'm also a very deadline-driven author, which is to say, I need external motivation. Guilt, the need for cash—those work really well for me.

What's the most important thing you've learned as a writer?

To make peace with my crazy process, and not to compare it with any other writer's process. As long as you reach the peak of the mountain, the path you take is irrelevant. Whatever works.

What is most rewarding to you about writing?

I love working for myself, surprising myself with something I've written when I read it months later and think, wow, did I come

up with that? I also love speaking to teenagers and hearing how a book touched them or made them laugh or got them through a difficult time. There are so many rewards from writing. It's hard to pare it down. I love it all!

What's your best advice for people who want to write for teens?

Remember that teens are—pause for collective gasp—just people. They are you, they are me, they are all of us. They're just younger. Don't be a separatist. Give them more credit for their insightfulness, sophistication, and intelligence. They are critically thinking, bright, open individuals and deserve fiction that respects all of that in them.

Q&A

James Van Pelt

www.sff.net/people/james.van.pelt
Blog: jimvanpelt.livejournal.com

Published books:

Strangers and Beggars
The Last of the O-Forms and Other Stories
Summer of the Apocalypse

Please say a few words about the YA subgenre in which you write.

I've never specifically set out to write for the YA crowd. However, I'm a longtime high school English teacher who loves his work, so I frequently use schools as a setting and young adults as my protagonists. Also, I have a deeply ingrained PG-13 sensibility at worst, so young adults have found my works and enjoyed them. Most of my stories are science fiction or fantasy, with an occasional foray into horror. I don't believe there is a particularly special writing challenge in working in those genres, if the writer's mind naturally turns that way. I look at situations and have a tendency to imagine science fictional or fantasy "what ifs." For example, one day I noticed a black widow had made a nest in a hard-to-reach corner of my classroom that was right behind my podium. Every time I got close to it, it would vanish into a crack between the sheetrock and the carpet. I tried spraying it several times, but it would not die. Since I'm a little arachnophobic, this bothered me. I imagined the spider creeping up on me as I was talking, so I could be in the middle of a lecture, and then suddenly pirouette, thinking the bug was moving toward me. Eventually I started to think, what if the spider never died, but kept getting larger instead?

Out of that "what if" came a fantasy/horror story about a truly large spider in a classroom, called "Miss Hathaway's Spider." The special challenge for me would be to write a western or a detective story. My mind doesn't tend that way.

How many rejections have you received in the course of your writing career? How did you deal with being rejected?

Rejection is a part of the writing business. I started sending short stories out with the hopes of publishing in 1984, but I didn't sell one until 1990. Some stories have sold to the first place that I sent them, but most have seen more than one publisher. The most rejections I have on a single story that eventually sold was 49. It circulated in the mail for ten years before finding a home at a magazine that didn't even exist when I started submitting it. The key is to be persistent. I tried selling stories for six years without succeeding once. Now, seventeen years later, I've sold over 90 stories and three books.

What's your approach to finishing a book?

Finishing a book is pretty much like finishing a short story, but it takes longer to get there. I'm the kind of writer who does not outline, and I frequently do not know the end of the story when I start (most of the writers I know write this way—the outliners are a rarer crowd). Somewhere during the middle, though, the end becomes clear to me, and I can push toward it with confidence. When I don't know the end of the story, or even the next sentence, I trust that something will occur to me. Another writer once said that writing a novel is just like driving across the country at night. Your headlights only show you thirty feet of road, but you can go thousands of miles that way before arriving at your destination.

What's the most important thing you've learned as a writer?

I tell my students that all that is necessary to be a writer is to be able to observe, to have a felicity with language, to be able to

make connections, and to have something to say. But that's really four things, not one. If I had to stick to just one lesson that has impacted me as a writer it would be to be specific. Ferociously, insanely specific. Everything else will fall into place if I remember that writing, like life, is all in the details.

What is most rewarding to you about writing?

I'd like to say it is the groupies, but most writers don't attract rock and roll fame. What I like about writing is that I can continue to do what I did as a child: make up stories and live in imaginary worlds.

What's your best advice for people who want to write for teens?

That's a good question because "teens" are not exactly a group that has similar tastes. I can say how not to write for teens: Don't write "down" to them. Don't patronize. Don't dummy anything. Write vividly about people doing real things, and the teens will find you.

A more practical answer, but certainly not true in all cases, is that stories with teen protagonists are frequently interesting to teens. The tough thing about writing for teens, though, is that a lot of teen life, "real" teen life, is not school safe. Teens are young adults, with the key word there being "adults."

Q&A

Denise Vega
www.denisevega.com

Published books:

Click Here (To Find Out How I Survived Seventh Grade)
Fact of Life #31

Please say a few words about the YA subgenre in which you write.

I write contemporary fiction, where I do my best to reflect the lives and truths of today's teens authentically. I draw from my own middle school and high school experiences (which were often painful and sometimes humiliating!) and I'm lucky enough to be around lots of teens to observe and talk about their experiences. I like to balance my pathos with a little humor, though, because if we can't laugh, we're doomed.

How many rejections have you received in the course of your writing career? How did you deal with being rejected?

Too many to count! Each rejection or "decline" as the wonderful author Claudia Mills calls them, can feel personal because I've worked so hard on a book—how can someone not love it as much as I do? But over the years I've come to recognize that decisions can be very subjective and that this is also a business. This particular publisher doesn't think it can sell my product in the marketplace so I need to find that one who does. The important thing is to get that manuscript back out to the next editor I think is right for the book—unless it needs work. If the editor has taken the time to com-

AUTHOR Q&A

ment on my work, I always consider the comments carefully to see whether I agree with them and need to revise. It's amazing what a little time away from a manuscript can do for my perspective! I almost always revise a rejected manuscript before sending it out again, whether I received comments from an editor or not.

My best antidote for dealing with rejection is throwing darts at pictures of editors who've sent me such a horrid thing—kidding. Actually, I allow myself about five minutes of wallowing in self-pity, and then I decide if the manuscript needs to be revised or if it can go out again as is to the next publisher on the list. Once I do that, I get to work on my current project. I always have another book I'm working on that I'm in love with. That's the secret to not going crazy in this business: working on something that is fun and that you're passionate about while you wait for responses from manuscripts that are out with publishers.

What's your approach to finishing a book?

Crossing my fingers, begging the literary gods for help, and eating lots of chocolate. Seriously, finishing a book for me means getting through the first draft, which is difficult because I tend to write by the seat of my pants. I get lost or come to a complete halt partway through. Recently I've done more planning—writing out bits of scenes and dialogue in some semblance of order, making sure I know the emotional growth arc for my main character, understanding where I want to end up—before I actually begin writing the first draft. I also try to resist the urge to go back and "fix" things as I write. If something comes up that I want to add or change, I make a note of it and keep going rather than take care of it right then. After I've revised the first draft about a zillion times, I offer it up to my critique group who slices, dices, and mixes it up into an unrecognizable blob that I must then reshape into something that resembles a decent book. I revise several more times until I feel it's ready to send to my agent so she can get it out to one of my publishers. Then I celebrate this milestone with something yummy!

What's the most important thing you've learned as a writer?

That the only thing in my control is the quality of the work. Everything else—getting the book accepted, how the publisher markets it (or doesn't—we midlist authors have to do a lot of our own marketing), book reviews, what readers think—is out of my control. The only thing I can do is write the best book I possibly can at the time, which for me means constantly improving my craft through reading YA lit, writing and revising, revising, revising. It's important to remember that revising isn't about moving a sentence or deleting a word here or there. It's about revisioning the entire work—seeing it in a new way so you can really make the changes necessary to improve it.

What is most rewarding to you about writing?

Creating characters and situations that readers can relate to and hearing from readers about how the book moved them, made them laugh, caused them to behave differently in a situation than they would have before reading the book. Books have changed my attitudes about relationships and situations, and if at least one reader was touched by something I wrote, then all of the effort to get the book out there was worth it. I'm lucky to have heard from many readers who have enjoyed and been moved by my work.

What's your best advice for people who want to write for teens?

Don't be afraid. If you want to try something edgy, go for it. If you want to write a story with a spiritual or religious angle, do it. Teens come from a variety of backgrounds and experiences and teen lit has room to reflect all their different realities. Write what you're excited about, not about what you think is the latest trend or what a publisher might want. In the end, it's just you and the page. Fill it with something that matters to you.

* * * * *

Ahhh. Now that you've been entertained and informed by eloquent folks with a passion to write fiction for young adults, imagine taking your own place among them. These interviews prove there isn't just one way to go about writing teen literature—there are as many ways as there are people writing.

Writing
EXERCISES

Final challenge. Imagine wading into the river of time and moving into the future. See yourself as a published writer. Now ask your future self to answer the interview questions that follow. Just allow the answers to come forth. Don't worry about whether you believe they'll come true.

*   Please say a few words about the YA subgenre in which you write.
*   How many rejections have you received in the course of your writing career? How did you deal with being rejected?
*   What's your approach to finishing a book?
*   What's the most important thing you've learned as a writer?
*   What is most rewarding to you about writing?
*   What's your best advice for people who want to write for teens?

The End

Writing a book is such a journey. If this were fiction, it would be time to check in with the characters one last time. I'd be looking back to the first chapter and all that had happened since it began. Nonfiction is different. Instead of the presence of characters, I've imagined readers beside me, chapter by chapter. And now that the book is done, I don't really like saying good-bye.

So I'll look forward to meeting you again in the form of an excellent novel. Written by you.

ACKNOWLEDGMENTS

Great thanks to Cheri Thurston for being an awesome editor with just the right mixture of nitpicky knowledge, intuitive understanding, and super humor. Thanks also to Samantha Prust, for relentless attention to detail combined with a warm personal style; to Sarah Stimely for her quiet expertise applied behind the scenes; to Anne Marie Martinez for her great patience designing the cover; and to the other members of Cottonwood Press for all their work on behalf of this book. What a dedicated and talented bunch! And thanks also to Pat Howard for painting the cover art.

Big gratitude to my husband Tim, who put up with all the weekends and holidays I spent writing. You're the best, Tim, and I thank you with everything I am for your easy patience and ever-loving kindness.

Thanks to my kids, Emrys and Rose, for being a perpetual source of inspiration and the gleam in my eye.

Thanks to all the teens who have bought and read my books—special thanks to those who have sent e-mails. Thanks also to workshop participants far and wide, for providing buckets of fun and motivation.

Gratitude beyond measure for my friends who have hung in there with me even when I disappeared for months at a time during the writing of this book. Over-the-top prize goes to Rebecca, who met me at a coffee shop on Christmas Day to go over our respective chapters. Rebecca, let's not tell the shrinks about that meeting, okay?

To the Thursday word wenches, you are marvelous and talented and I miss your company. Maryjo, the thought of your smile and gavel-banging have carried me through many a too-long day.

Thanks to Diane Tuccillo, Sue-Ellen Jones, and Mary McCarthy, who used their skills as teen librarians to assist me with reference questions, and their skills as remarkable human beings to bring a sense of possibility to this project.

And to all the wonderful writers, editors, and agents who contributed interviews for this book—thank you for your time, your expertise, and your help.

ABOUT THE AUTHOR

Victoria Hanley is an award-winning author of young adult fiction published in ten languages. She lives in Loveland, Colorado.

To learn more, visit her website:

www.victoriahanley.com